POLITICS AND TYRANNY

Lessons in the Pursuit of Freedom

D1617616

POLITICS AND TYRANNY
Lessons in the Pursuit of Freedom

Milton Friedman et al.

Edited with an introduction by David J. Theroux

Pacific Institute for Public Policy Research
San Francisco, California

ISBN 0-936488-00-x
Library of Congress Catalog Card Number 84–061364

Printed in the United States of America

Pacific Institute for Public Policy Research
177 Post Street
San Francisco, California 94108

PACIFIC INSTITUTE

FOR PUBLIC POLICY RESEARCH

The Pacific Institute for Public Policy Research is an independent, tax-exempt research and educational organization. The Institute's program is designed to broaden public understanding of the nature and effects of market processes and government policy.

With the bureaucratization and politicization of modern society, scholars, business and civic leaders, the media, policymakers, and the general public have too often been isolated from meaningful solutions to critical public issues. To facilitate a more active and enlightened discussion of such issues, the Pacific Institute sponsors in-depth studies into the nature of and possible solutions to major social, economic, and environmental problems. Undertaken regardless of the sanctity of any particular government program, or the customs, prejudices, or temper of the times, the Institute's studies aim to ensure that alternative approaches to currently problematic policy areas are fully evaluated, the best remedies discovered, and these findings made widely available. The results of this work are published as books and monographs, and form the basis for numerous conference and media programs.

Through this program of research and commentary, the Institute seeks to evaluate the premises and consequences of government policy, and provide the foundations necessary for constructive policy reform.

PACIFIC STUDIES IN PUBLIC POLICY

Resolving the Housing Crisis
Government Policy, Decontrol, and the Public Interest
Edited with an Introduction by M. Bruce Johnson

Offshore Lands
Oil and Gas Leasing and the Environment on the Outer Continental Shelf
By Walter J. Mead, et al.
Foreword by Stephen L. McDonald

Electric Power
Deregulation and the Public Interest
Edited by John C. Moorhouse
Foreword by Harold Demsetz

Taxation and the Deficit Economy
Fiscal Policy and Capital Formation in the United States
Edited by Dwight R. Lee
Foreword by Michael J. Boskin

The American Family and the State
Edited by Joseph R. Peden and Fred R. Glahe

Dealing With Drugs
Problems of Government Control
Edited by Ronald L. Hamowy

Crisis and Leviathan
Critical Episodes in the Growth of American Government
By Robert Higgs
Foreword by Arthur A. Ekirch, Jr.

FORTHCOMING

The New China
Comparative Economic Development in Hong Kong, Taiwan, and Mainland China

Political Business Cycles
The Economics and Politics of Stagflation

Rationing Health Care
Medical Licensing in the United States

Crime, Police, and the Courts

Myth and Reality in Social Welfare

Health Care Delivery Institutions

Rent Control in Santa Monica

Health Insurance: Public and Private

Unemployment and the State

For further information on the Pacific Institute's program and a catalog of publications, please contact:

PACIFIC INSTITUTE FOR PUBLIC POLICY RESEARCH
177 Post Street
San Francisco, California 94108

Contents

Introduction

David J. Theroux

Economist and former *Newsweek* columnist Henry Wallich has credited Milton Friedman with having "almost single-handedly" changed economic thinking on the subject of money.[1] Indeed, Milton Friedman, the 1976 Nobel laureate in economic science, is a world renowned economist and an academician of the finest caliber. But he is much more. He is an articulate and persuasive advocate of individual freedom, and the private property, voluntary exchange economy, which is based upon and sustains that freedom. British Prime Minister Margaret Thatcher has stated, "Professor Friedman is usually referred to as a monetarist, but his basic belief is not in money. It's in people's inherent right and ability to choose how they will live."

Milton Friedman was born July 31, 1912, in Brooklyn, New York. His parents, Sarah Ethel (Landau) and Jeno Saul Friedman, were poor immigrants born in Carpatho-Rumania, then a province of Austria-Hungary and currently part of the Soviet Union. When he was but a year old, the family moved to Rahway, New Jersey, where both his mother and his father were merchants.[2]

Friedman graduated from Rahway High School in 1928 and worked his way through Rutgers University, studying under Arthur Burns and Homer Jones. Burns shaped his understanding of economic research, and Jones

---

1. John Davenport, "The Radical Economics of Milton Friedman," *Fortune*, 1 June 1967, p. 131.
2. "Milton Friedman," *Current Biography 1969* (Bronx, NY: H. W. Wilson Co.), p. 151.

1

introduced him to rigorous economic theory. Intending to become an actuary, Friedman initially specialized in mathematics, but shortly developed an even stronger interest in economics. He eventually majored in both fields, graduating in 1932. On Jones's recommendation, the Department of Economics at the University of Chicago offered Friedman a graduate scholarship, which he accepted over a scholarship in applied mathematics at Brown University.[3]

In 1932 Friedman began graduate work at the University of Chicago, studying under such renowned economists as Frank Knight, Jacob Viner, and Henry Simons, who were in the process of forming what later came to be called the "Chicago School of Economics."[4] The Chicago School has since revolutionized the economics profession by its exacting use of empirical analysis and its rigorous and creative application of microeconomics throughout economic research and in fields once considered independent, such as law, sociology, history, and others.

While at Chicago, in the midst of the depression, Milton Friedman met Rose Director, sister of the distinguished economist Aaron Director. They were married six years later.

After receiving his M.A. in economics in 1933, Friedman accepted an attractive fellowship at Columbia University where, under Howard Hotelling, he acquired training in mathematical economics and statistics. After one year he returned to Chicago to assist Henry Shultz, who was then completing his classic *The Theory and Measurement of Demand*. From 1935 to 1937 he was an economist with the National Resources Planning Board in Washington, D.C., and in the fall of 1937 Friedman joined Simon Kuznets in the latter's studies of professional income at the National Bureau of Economic Research.

From 1940 to 1941 Friedman briefly returned to academia as a visiting professor of economics at the University of Wisconsin.[5] He spent 1941 to 1943 at the U.S. Department of Treasury working on wartime tax policy, and from 1943 to 1945 as a mathematical statistician working on problems of weapon design at Columbia University.[6]

In 1945 he joined George Stigler, who was later to become a fellow

3. "Milton Friedman," *Les Prix Nobel en 1976* (Stockholm: The Nobel Foundation, 1977), p. 239.
4. Karl Brunner, "The 1976 Nobel Prize in Economics," *Science* 194 (November 5, 1976), p. 595.
5. *Current Biography*, p. 152.
6. *Les Prix Nobel en 1976*, pp. 240–41.

Nobel laureate, at the University of Minnesota. A year later he was appointed associate professor of economics at the University of Chicago.

After completing his Ph.D. at Columbia in 1946, Friedman reworked his dissertation on professional licensure into a book coauthored with Kuznets, *Income from Independent Professional Practice.*[7] He then agreed to take responsibility for research into the role of money in the business cycle for the National Bureau of Economic Research.[8]

He spent the fall of 1950 in Paris as a consultant to the U.S. Marshall Plan. From 1953 to 1954 he was a Fulbright visiting professor at Cambridge University, where the economics faculty was deeply divided over Keynesian policies.[9] In 1956 he edited a collection of essays published as *Studies in the Quantity Theory of Money.* His introductory essay for that volume, "The Quantity Theory: A Restatement," resurrected the quantity theory as a viable alternative to Keynesian orthodoxy. With that he became known as the "father of monetarism," the school of economics that believes the amount of money in circulation is the dominant factor in the determination of nominal aggregate demand.

In 1959 his seminal work, *A Theory of the Consumption Function*, was published. This volume, which distinguishes between permanent and transitory income, together with his 1961 paper coauthored by David Meiselman, "The Relative Stability of Monetary Velocity and the Investment Multiplier in the United States," stirred a profound controversy in the economics profession.[10]

Friedman's research into the long, unpredictable lags between changes in the money supply and changes in real economic activity and inflation has led him to conclude that the only macroeconomic policy that will consistently yield desirable results is a slow, steady, predictable rate of growth of the money supply. This prescription, "monetarism," has been implemented to a much greater extent in Japan and Germany than elsewhere, and those countries have experienced lower rates of unemployment and inflation than countries whose monetary authorities have attempted otherwise.

Throughout the 1950s Friedman stayed clear of partisan politics and

---

7. *Current Biography*, p. 152.
8. *Les Prix Nobel en 1976*, p. 241.
9. Ibid.
10. *Current Biography*, p. 152.

concentrated on his work in positive economics. However, in 1962, with the help of Rose Friedman, he published his first major book in political philosophy, *Capitalism and Freedom*. In addition, he took an active interest in the highly influential classical liberal journal, *The New Individualist Review*, edited by then University of Chicago libertarian scholars Ralph Raico and Ronald Hamowy, each of whom completed his Ph.D. under Nobel laureate Friedrich A. Hayek.[11]

In 1963 his magnum opus (with Anna J. Schwartz), *A Monetary History of the United States, 1867–1960*, was published. This book more than any other forced the economics profession to take monetarism seriously. Friedman and Schwartz assembled convincing evidence in support of the view that all major macroeconomic crises in American history, especially the Great Depression, were caused by substantial monetary shocks. Government, not the free market, caused (and perpetuated) the Great Depression!

Friedman's analysis of the roles of information costs and inflation expectations in labor markets and his hypothesis of a natural rate of unemployment undermined one of the major pillars in the Keynesian orthodoxy—the Phillips curve. Because of Friedman's work and the work of others he inspired, by the late 1970s it could reasonably be said that true Keynesians no longer existed.

In all, Friedman is the author or co-author of more than 20 books and of roughly 100 scholarly papers for professional journals, plus numerous other articles and reviews for a wide range of popular publications. He was the Paul Snowden Russell Distinguished Service Professor of Economics at the University of Chicago until his retirement from active teaching in 1977, when he joined the Hoover Institution at Stanford University as a senior research fellow. He continues to be a member of the research staff at the National Bureau of Economic Research and, until recently, was a contributing editor and columnist for *Newsweek* magazine.

Like F. A. Hayek, Friedman is an unabashed classical liberal who does not accept the label "conservative" because of his view that it connotes blind acceptance of the past. He clearly perceives and teaches the interdependence of economic freedom with the civil liberties of free speech, worship, press, assembly, and so forth. Consequently, he is one of the

11. Milton Friedman, "Introduction," *New Individualist Review* (Indianapolis: Liberty Press, 1981), pp. ix–xiv.

most eloquent and persuasive advocates of the economic and ethical superiority of free markets over collectivist government control.

In the course of his defense of individual freedom, Friedman has been the architect or advocate of many influential and ingenious proposals to resolve critical public issues, while at the same time dismantling government bureaucracy. Among his proposals are the following:

Negative Income Tax: To eliminate the massive welfare system's disincentives and enormous waste, abolish all welfare programs and replace them with a program of direct cash payments to those actually in need simply by adding a new income tax bracket (one for negative values of taxable income) to the tax code.

Educational Voucher: To provide a competitive climate for public and private education, all parents of primary and secondary school children would be issued government vouchers to be spent at the school of their choice. Government's only role would be to provide the vouchers; competition for clients would assure quality and innovation.

Flat Income Tax: To streamline the tax system and to lower its enormous direct costs to the general public and the indirect inefficiencies imposed on the economy, abolish the corporate income tax. Instead, tax individuals only at a nonprogressive flat rate, raising personal exemptions to some minimum income level and ending all loopholes.

Stable Money Growth: To eliminate the recurring problems of inflation, unemployment, and decreased productivity, abolish the Federal Reserve System, legalize private monies, and peg the increase of the government money supply to the growth in GNP, perhaps 0 to 3 percent per year.

Floating Exchange Rates: To solve the nation's balance-of-payments problems and to open the possibility of unilaterally eliminating anti-consumer protectionist measures, abolish exchange controls and let national currencies seek their own price levels in the market.

Balanced Budget: Since deficit spending is simply a device for hiding tax increases, thereby lowering taxpayer resistance to government spending and impairing economic growth, all government spending should be handled according to the merits of each specific proposal on a pay-as-you-go basis. Fiscal policy should never be used to affect business cycles, and the Balanced Budget Amendment should be adopted.

Volunteer Army: To create a more efficient, better motivated, and morally tenable defense system, abolish the compulsory servitude of the draft and draft registration and maintain a voluntary system of enlistment based on competitive benefits and professional, career-oriented training.

No Victimless Crime Laws: To direct limited police and legal resources to the problems of violent crime, eliminate all laws creating crimes with no victims. More specifically, where consent is present between two or more adults no injustice can be possible; hence government has no place in proscribing or regulating such areas as prostitution, pornography, drugs, and so forth. Moreover, Friedman would agree with Harvard philosopher Robert Nozick's position that such practices should be equally legal along with all "capitalist acts between consenting adults." [12]

As a result of his devotion to individual freedom, Friedman was an early and vocal supporter of California's Proposition 13 to reduce property taxes across-the-board, as well as President Reagan's original proposal to cut individual and corporate income tax rates. He is opposed to farm price supports, securities and exchange controls, and, in fact, all government interventions into the peaceful pursuits of individuals. To Friedman, government's role should be stringently restricted to defending the nation from foreign enemies, defending persons from force and fraud, providing a forum for decisions on the general rules determining property and similar rights, and providing a means to mediate disputes about the rules.

Perhaps Friedman's greatest success began in 1979 when he and his wife Rose produced the book *Free to Choose*, based on the now famous ten-part TV series for PBS by the same title. Both the TV program and the book were drawn from an earlier series of lectures presented by Friedman. Because it aired during a period of critical economic distress, the program is widely regarded as being a major factor in shifting American public opinion toward appreciating the need to dismantle government largess. The series has since been shown in England, Japan, Australia, Canada, and other countries, and the book has been translated for distribution around the world.

As a result of his impact on academic and public opinion, Friedman has been an economic advisor to Presidents Ronald Reagan, Gerald Ford, and Richard Nixon, as well as Prime Minister Margaret Thatcher. But to this day, he has consistently turned down full-time positions in government, preferring to continue his scientific work and leave public activities to full-time policymakers.

12. "Portrait: Milton Friedman," *Challenge* (May–June 1978), p. 69; Milton Friedman, *Capitalism and Freedom* (Chicago: University of Chicago Press, 1962); and Milton and Rose Friedman, *Free to Choose* (New York: Harcourt Brace Jovanovich, 1980).

Now living in San Francisco, the Friedmans have two children: David, who currently teaches economics at Tulane University in New Orleans, and Janet, who practices law in Davis, California.

To recognize the enormous contributions of this man, the Pacific Institute sponsored the National Dinner to Honor Milton Friedman on October 4, 1983, in San Francisco. Seven hundred individuals from across the United States assembled to pay tribute to this champion of freedom and economic scholarship. The Honorary National Chairman for the program was former Secretary of the Treasury William E. Simon, and the Dinner Committee was co-chaired by J. Peter Grace (chairman, W. R. Grace and Company), George M. Keller (chairman, Standard Oil Company of California), and Robert H. Malott (chairman, FMC Corporation). We are sincerely grateful for the splendid assistance of each, along with the entire dinner committee.

This volume assembles the major remarks from that historic event, including the address by Professor Friedman entitled "Tyranny of the Status Quo," plus a detailed bibliography of his many publications. The Pacific Institute is very pleased and honored to have made this lasting tribute possible.

DINNER COMMITTEE
William E. Simon
Honorary Chairman
J. Peter Grace, George M. Keller, Robert H. Malott
Dinner Co-Chairmen

Jerome A. Adams
Joseph F. Alibrandi
Poul Anderson
Roy A. Anderson
William S. Anderson
Ernest C. Arbuckle
Samuel H. Armacost
Hon. Anne Armstrong
George T. Ballou
Norman Barker, Jr.
John B. Bates
William M. Batten
S. D. Bechtel, Jr.
Bernice W. Behrens
Everett E. Berg
William Blackie
Winton M. Blount
D. P. Boothe, Jr.
David A. Bossen
R. J. Boyd
Mr. and Mrs. William S. Boyd
William H. Brady, Jr.
Robert S. Brickell
William H. Bricker
James R. Bronkema
Charles H. Brunie
Karl Brunner
John H. Bryan, Jr.
James F. Buckley, Jr.
William F. Buckley, Jr.
Robert D. Burnham
Robert W. Busch
Nolan K. Bushnell
Preston Butcher
John R. Cahill
Paul W. Cane
Danielle Carlisle
Robert J. Carlson
John B. Carter
Christopher Casler
Clive Chandler
A. Lawrence Chickering
Robert J. Chitester
Howard L. Clark
Joseph E. Coberly, Jr.
Dorman L. Commons
Joseph Coors
Mr. and Mrs. Herbert C. Cornuelle
William T. Creson
Charles Crocker
Lester Crown
Edwin F. Cutler
Douglas D. Danforth
Carl F. Danielson
Stuart Davis
Charles de Bretteville
Frederick B. Dent
William A. Diehl
Phyllis Diller
Gaylord Donnelley
Thomas E. Drohan
Myron Du Bain
Ronald E. Eadie
Edwin J. Feulner, Jr.

Mr. and Mrs. Antony G. A. Fisher
Donald G. Fisher
Richard J. Flamson, III
R. A. Flohr
J. R. Fluor
Alfred Fromm
Robert W. Galvin
Charles C. Gates
Anthony T. C. Gaw
Peter Goldman
Charles L. Gould
John P. Greene
Alan Greenspan
Donald E. Guinn
Prentis Cobb Hale
Ralph O. Hanley
John D. Harper
James R. Harvey
Calvin S. Hatch
K. Courtenay Hawkins, Jr.
Friedrich A. Hayek
Mrs. Antonia Hayes
Walter E. Hoadley
Bob Hope
Matina S. Horner
Gordon L. Hough
Jerome W. Hull
Jacquelin H. Hume
James F. Hurley
Samuel H. Husbands, Jr.
Robert S. Ingersoll
George D. Jagels
Amos A. Jordan
Robert W. Kerr
Mr and Mrs. Franklin J. Keville
David H. Keyston
Alton H. Kingman, Jr.
Charles G. Koch
David H. Koch
Herbert V. Kohler, Jr.
Robert H. Krieble
S. W. Kung
J. Clayburn LaForce, Jr.
Lewis Lehrman
Donald D. Lennox
Werner Lewin
Drew Lewis
Ernest J. Loebbecke
Graham Loving
Charles A. Lynch
Richard B. Madden
Cyril Magnin
Henry G. Manne
Fritz Maytag
John A. McCone
Henry W. Meers
Hon. Edwin Meese, III
David I. Meiselman
Arnold Michaels
Buck Mickel
Frederick W. Mielke, Jr.
Dr. William F. Miller
James F. Montgomery
H. B. Morley

Richard M. Morrow
Senator Daniel Patrick Moynahan
John J. Nevin
James D. North
Robert Nozick
Francis A. O'Connell
Walter E. Ousterman, Jr.
David Packard
Thomas C. Paton
Congressman Ron Paul
Rudolph A. Peterson
Charles M. Pigott
John B. M. Place
L. John Polite, Jr.
Robert Poole, Jr.
Edmund T. Pratt, Jr.
Randall E. Presley
Leland S. Prussia
Michael G. Rafton
A. M. Regalia
Jack L. Richardson
John M. Richman
Robert Ringer
Trevor C. Roberts
David Rockefeller
Arthur Rubloff
Louis Rukeyser
Donald Rumsfeld
Philip S. Schlein
Edward Schultz
Anna J. Schwartz
Arnold Schwarzenegger
David C. Scott
Walter D. Scott
John S. R. Shad
J. Gary Shansby
Mark Shepherd, Jr.
Walter H. Shorenstein
Mr. and Mrs. J. R. Simplot
William D. Smithburg
Mrs. Ji Ing Soong
Hon. Beryl W. Sprinkel
Robert L. Sproull
Norbert Stanislav
Jeffery D. Stein
D. R. Stephens
Samuel Stewart
George J. Stigler
Martin Stone
Paul Stone
Frederick P. Stratton, Jr.
Robert E. Thomas
Governor James R. Thompson
Lewis K. Uhler
T. Urling Walker
Rawleigh Warner, Jr.
Robert B. Wilhelm
Senator Pete Wilson
William M. Witter
Walter B. Wriston
William T. Ylvisaker
Efrem Zimbalist, Jr.

PART I

Milton Friedman:
Champion of Freedom

1. A Social Perspective

Benjamin Stein

When I told my "Valley Girl" assistant that I was coming up here tonight, she asked why. "To honor Milton Friedman," I said. "Oh, Milton Friedman," she said. "He's that full-on braino who tells presidents what to do, right?" Right, but he is much more than that.

Friedman is a name to conjure with for my entire life. My parents knew him, and knew him well. They knew that he was the absolute last word on any question of economics, and that if there were a dispute about an economic subject, no rebuttals really mattered until they heard what Milton Friedman had to say, and then that would be the end of it.

It wasn't until I left home and went to Columbia University that I realized there is an enormously important other side to Professor Friedman, and it wasn't until I was there for some time that I realized Professor Friedman was, and is, a dangerous man in the very best sense of that word. Let me explain.

About twenty years ago, I was sitting in a dismal and miserable chair in a library at Columbia, reading a book, and the book began, "Ask not what your country can do for you, but what you can do for your country." And I thought, "Oh boy, here's some other guy who's going to start screaming and salivating about John F. Kennedy," and then, to my shock, the author wrote, "In a free society, neither is a worthy question to ask of a free people." I thought, "Wait a minute. This is not the usual stuff." This was my first inkling that Professor Friedman was a dangerous man, and I learned my first basic truth about him—that no cliche, no banality, no truism, no seeming axiom of the status quo is safe when he is around.

A few days later, I had the good fortune to attend one of Professor Friedman's lectures at which a student blithely raised her hand and said, "Well, what about raising taxes so we can have better free state universities?" Professor Friedman stopped her right there and said, "Why should we have free state universities at all? Why should we tax the son of the sharecropper to pay for music appreciation for the son of the surgeon?" Everyone in the class was dumbfounded. So was I, and I realized again that Professor Friedman had struck in his usual deadly way. He is a dangerous man. There is no holy of holies too holy to escape his notice and no sacred cow too safe to be slaughtered.

In the twenty years since then I have seen one icon after another tremble and fall before the onslaught of this dangerous man: Should we have tariffs to protect the industry that makes TV sets? Why should we? Why not let the Japanese work for us for low wages if they want to? Should we hate and fear sweatshops? Maybe they teach immigrants how to work in disciplined surroundings. Maybe they do something that is very rare nowadays—give people a chance to have the dignity of earning their own living. Should we worry about our public schools? Should we pump more and more money into them? Maybe not. Maybe we should let the students decide where they get the best education by a voucher system. Always something new, always something unexpected, always something dangerous.

I propose to you that Professor Friedman—a man who is an almost unrivaled genius in mathematics, a man who has explained the unexplainable in economic theory time after time—has done even more in the realms of political philosophy and in understanding basically what human beings are about. He is tireless; he is brilliant; he is utterly original. He surveys the whole landscape of modern life, and to every aspect of that life he asks a few simple crucial questions: Does this show confidence in man as a free being? Does this increase or diminish man's range of choice, man's control over his destiny? Does this reward man for his energy and his discipline, or does it punish him? Is this an act worthy of a free people in a free society?

Only as short a time as twenty years ago, Professor Friedman and a small group of men and women were virtually alone asking those crucial questions. But little by little, gradually and then swiftly, those questions have become the watchwords of a large part of the American people, a large part of both political parties, and I'm happy to say, of a president.

By his example, by the beautiful, elegant proofs in his books, in his television shows, in his articles, he has brought an entire nation back to the founding principles revealed in the questions he posed.

This is a man of genius, praised even by his bitterest ideological enemies for his unfailing courtesy and thoughtfulness, and he has reminded a nation that has too long been adrift of what it is all about. He is in that way dangerous to anyone who forgets the meaning of a free society.

This is a man who has traveled all over the world to countries with and without a long tradition of freedom, and he has explained to their peoples why freedom and the dignity of the individual—not an overpowering state—offer the best and the surest way to prosperity and stability. He travels all over the world and he repeats again and again one crucial theme: the dignity of the free human spirit is the fountain from which everything good and fine and lasting flows. In that sense, also, he is dangerous to anyone on earth who fears freedom.

Even in the United Kingdom—the undisputed cradle of individual freedom—after a long period of sad drift, they, too, turned to Professor Friedman to get that needed course correction. Anywhere in the world, from Singapore to Jerusalem to London to Sacramento to Washington—anywhere the message of human dignity and individual freedom needs to be heard—Professor Friedman has been there, and I suspect he will be there again.

This is a kind of obsession, and it has led people to call him inflexible and single-minded. For my own part, and I think I share the feelings of most of the people in this room, I can hardly think of anything more wonderful to say about an American than that he is inflexible and single-minded in his devotion to the cause of freedom.

If I may now be permitted an idiosyncratic moment (as opposed to all those other moments), I personally—and I speak for my parents and for my wife, as well, and I think for everyone who knows Professor Friedman—have been extremely impressed for as long as I've known him, that this man who advises presidents and premiers and cabinets and, I suppose, some kings are in there, too, is in person the most unassuming, unpretentious, gentle man one can imagine. The most miserable graduate student assistant in economics at the most miserable community college approaches the students with more arrogance than does Professor Friedman. I have seen many famous and many ordinary men and women argue with Professor Friedman, and I have often seen them lose their temper and become mocking and bitter, struggling against the insurmountable rock of his ability. But I have never seen Professor Friedman lose his temper; I've never seen him grow impolite, even when arguing with the most mean-spirited opponents—and he is so able and so overwhelming in debate, that his opponents often, out of desperation, do become mean-spirited.

He is a man who gives a whole new meaning to words like confidence, humility, and gentlemanliness in his bearing and in his demeanor. He is a man, in other words, to be admired for his personality and for his heart, as well as for his beliefs and for his genius. Luckily for those of us in this room and for all the people who believe in the individual and in freedom, he has used that personality, that genius, that ability, that persistence, to do something basic and crucial: he pulled this nation back to the paths of its beginning. On television, in print, in person, he says over and over again, "You are a free people, heirs to Jefferson and Madison. Are you working for that tradition or against that tradition? Is what you are doing yesterday and today and tomorrow going to make the rights of the individual stronger or weaker?" In everything he writes and speaks and does, Professor Friedman always says implicitly, "Remember what America is all about. Remember that always and everywhere—remember it, love it, and work to preserve it."

It is a great, great honor to join in tribute to a man who has been so vital in protecting the best of what this nation is and should be. Professor Friedman, you are a "full-on braino," but you are the braino and the dangerous man that a free people need.

2. An Academic Perspective

M. Bruce Johnson

I once knew an economist who claimed he could forecast the lifetime research of his fellow professionals by the following formula: $Q_1 \times Q_2 = c$; roughly translated, that means quantity times quality equals a constant— and small. Clearly, Milton Friedman's research record casts serious doubts on the empirical validity of this law. Milton Friedman is a special scholar whose numerous important contributions to economic analysis could not be listed, let alone adequately praised, in the few pages allocated to me here.

Thus, I shall briefly highlight two areas of Milton's research: monetary economics and consumption analysis. One should not infer, merely because I exclude specific reference to them, that I don't appreciate his contributions to price theory, expected utility, methodology, and exchange rate analysis—only some of the areas in which he has made major contributions.

Friedman's work in monetary economics spans the field from the history of money to the frontiers of theory. These works include: "The Quantity Theory of Money—A Restatement," in *Studies in the Quantity Theory of Money* (1956); *A Monetary History of the United States: 1867–1960*, with Anna Schwartz (1963); *The Optimum Quantity of Money* (1969); *Monetary Statistics of the United States*, with Anna Schwartz (1970); *Monetary Trends in the United States and the United Kingdom*, with Anna Schwartz (1982).

15

When I assert that Milton Friedman's work has redefined monetary history, reshaped monetary theory, and influenced monetary policy, I am guilty of understatement. Friedman is responsible for drawing attention, research, and debate to the causal role of the quantity of money (and its rates of change) as opposed to interest rates or other indicators of monetary conditions. His work has become the standard for all scholars in the field; those who agree with his conclusions and those who disagree all use his research as the starting point for their own investigations. Monumental is the best adjective to describe this work. It is impossible to imagine what the fields of monetary history, theory, and policy would be like without Milton's contributions.

A Theory of the Consumption Function was published in 1957. Here Friedman introduced the hypothesis that household consumption depends on long-run measures of income or wealth, rather than the current (or measured) income then used in the Keynesian formulations. The economic and statistical ideas at the heart of his Permanent Income Hypothesis quickly became the analytical standard in a wide variety of settings and applications. In addition, the book immediately resolved and illuminated a variety of formerly puzzling results from time-series and cross-section studies of household savings behavior. And the illumination was most brilliant in its execution and presentation.

A Theory of the Consumption Function is my favorite among Milton's many contributions to economic analysis. It is masterful, rich, subtle, and elegant. Furthermore, the book demonstrates his ability and willingness to write as lucidly for a technical audience as he later wrote for a general audience.

Milton Friedman has, above all, a profound sense of the possibilities and boundaries of empirical science. He is masterful at isolating the relevant features of an issue, just as he is at dismissing the trivial. He has given us many original and fruitful ideas; his work influences many of the questions asked, the analyses employed, and the empirical techniques used.

If you think I overstate the wisdom and vision of this scholar, let me share with you an old University of Chicago saying: "Milton is always right—he's sometimes a bit early."

Finally, I would like to quote from remarks by Karl Brunner in his American Economic Association address honoring the Nobel Laureate for 1976 (December 29, 1977):

Milton Friedman has powerfully contributed to a broad vision of economics and a sharper appreciation that economics is not about contrived problems but about the world we live in. We should understand that his intellectual thrust is directed toward the very center of contemporary confrontation. This thrust is, moreover, guided by scientific criteria that submit his ideas and the work of all others to searching examination in a competitive struggle for assessable knowledge. Friedman's work addresses fundamentally the institutions of an open society and the survival of freedom and human dignity.

It is a privilege to join in honoring a unique intellect, a scholar whose ideas have increased our understanding of human behavior and have guided our imperfect efforts at making public policy. Professor Milton Friedman, thank you!

3. A Business Perspective

George M. Keller

As I think many of you know, Milton Friedman was born in Brooklyn, New York. He has made a lot of trips since then. The first was when he was at about the age of one, to Rahway, New Jersey, then on to such places as Rutgers University, Columbia University, where he received his Ph.D. some thirty-seven years ago, the University of Chicago, where he is still playing a distinguished role, the U.S. Treasury, the Hoover Institution at Stanford, and so forth.

His influence on economic thinking in the United States and thinking around the world is incalculable. When Milton Friedman speaks or writes, he commands the attention of heads of state, business, civic, and religious leaders, as well as scholars. I would like to share with you a sampling of greetings to him from such figures.

Dear Milton:

I'm proud to join the Pacific Institute for Public Policy Research in honoring you on this special occasion.

The event presents me with the rare opportunity to pay tribute to a great man of intellect and a champion of liberty. You're a scholar of first rank whose original contributions to economic science have made you one of the greatest thinkers in modern history.

Not since the time of Adam Smith has such a finely focused mind concentrated on the intellectual underpinnings of a free society. Through such seminal works as *The Monetary History of the United States* and *Capitalism and Freedom*, and, of course, the widely acclaimed television series

19

"Free to Choose," you have played a major role in disseminating the philosophy of freedom across our land and around the world.

As the dean of the Chicago school of economics, you have expanded our knowledge and encouraged greater understanding of the crucial role of monetary policy in the lives of men and nations. Just as your selection for the Nobel Prize in Economics recognized your intellectual leadership, so we acknowledge your significant influence on the ongoing debate regarding public policy issues.

Congratulations on this well-deserved tribute and may your dream of a world where all will be 'free to choose' one day be a reality.

Sincerely,
Ronald Reagan

I have here a letter from the Office of the Mayor of the City of San Francisco:

Dear Mr. Theroux:

I am very pleased to learn that the Pacific Institute for Public Policy Research is honoring Nobel laureate Milton Friedman with a special dinner here in San Francisco on Tuesday, October 4.

All San Franciscans join me in warmly welcoming Professor Friedman to our City, and in sharing with him our sincere appreciation for his truly invaluable public services. Professor Friedman's long and distinguished career has made him one of the world's foremost economists and a legend in his own lifetime—accomplishments which have added significantly to overall public understanding of some of today's most complicated economic issues, and we are pleased to have access to them.

Have a wonderful dinner on Tuesday evening, and thank you again for your exemplary services to San Francisco.

Warm personal regards,
Sincerely,
Dianne Feinstein
Mayor of City and County of San Francisco

From the gentleman who has been our national honorary chairman for tonight's dinner, the following was written:

Dear Milton:

Carol and I are very disappointed that we can't be with you on October 4 to honor you at the Pacific Institute's dinner. Were it not for a long-scheduled commitment that evening, we would certainly be in San Francisco celebrating with you.

No one better deserves this honor than you do. You are a thoughtful and prolific scholar, a Nobel laureate. But your influence reaches far beyond the academic community and the world of economics. Rather than lock yourself in an ivory tower, you have joined the fray to fight for the survival of this great country of ours. Your courage, your steadfastness, and your integrity are an inspiration to the many Americans who are at your side in the battle.

As one of those Americans, I thank you for your extraordinary leadership over the past several decades. The wind has not always blown in our direction, but you have never wavered in your commitment to individual liberty.

If I were there with you, I would propose a toast to one of the greatest Americans of our day. May your calm voice of reason and good sense continue to be heard across this land; never has our country had greater need of your wisdom.

> With warmest regards, as always,
> William E. Simon

A sampling of telegrams include the following:

> Unable to arrive in time, I still wish to send Milton, old friend and comrade in arms for many years, all my most cordial wishes for his future work and health.
>
> Friedrich A. Hayek

> Congratulations and all good wishes to one of the brightest young economists in the business. You'll always be M−1 in my book.
>
> With the bullish best wishes of
> Louis Rukeyser

> Regret I cannot join you tonight to express how grateful I have been over the years for the cogency of your ideas which have so influenced me. Cherishers of freedom will be indebted to you for generations to come. My personal best to you and especially to Rose, the wisest person I know.
>
> Alan Greenspan

> I'm very grateful for your thoughtfulness in holding the national dinner to honor Milton Friedman. I'm a long and ardent admirer of his and I'm happy to know that this dinner is being given. But I deeply regret that the age and state of health of myself and my wife do not permit me to attend. I wish the dinner every success.
>
> Sincerely,
> Henry Hazlitt

And finally a very brief note from one of Milton's early and long-time friends and fellow Nobel laureate:

> To Milton Friedman: I wish I were attending the dinner at which California finally admits that you're a good economist. Indeed I hope that we both live long enough so I can attend a dinner given for you by the Federal Reserve Board. You do not believe in free meals, even for yourself, Milton, so give a good speech.

As you might guess, that's from George Stigler.

I would like to comment briefly about a particular experience that I remember, going back about five years. I had heard Milton Friedman speak on various occasions and had met him quite casually as part of fair-sized groups at one place or another, but had never really come to know this man.

Milton and I agreed to participate as commentators in a live British television program from San Francisco titled "North Sea Oil: Will We Be Rich?" It did not have anything to do with us, it really had to do with all those fine people in England and Scotland and Wales.

We sat on either side of a small table. We could hear the program from England, but we had no video of the proceedings at all—whichever one of us the light was on, the other side could see. It's a position I do not recommend anyone ever getting into. We did not even really know what specific questions or comments might be addressed to us. This was not something that was preprogrammed, other than we knew the general subject and we knew it was being controlled by independent television in the United Kingdom.

As it turned out, I was called on early in the show to discuss Chevron's role in the Ninian field, one of the very large North Sea developments. This gave me the opportunity to express my disappointment with the deteriorating U.K. tax and regulatory policy and particularly my frustration at the British National Oil Company, which was being imposed at this time on the private companies.

Lord Kirtin, the first chairman of British National Oil, happened to be one of the many participants on the stage in Britain, and he took considerable offense at my remarks. The rather acrimonious public debate may well have darkened U.S.–British relations, and maybe my corporation's future. But from time to time during this argument, Milton Friedman, a few feet away from me just off-camera, was cheering me on, "Give 'em hell, George, give 'em hell!" If I had been looking for a job as an assistant to an economist I might have come to see him soon after that.

Later in the program, Friedman showed how to restructure the socialist government's policies by suggesting that the tax and royalty income from North Sea oil production be distributed directly to the citizenry since they obviously would know far better than the government how to spend it. Needless to say, Tony Bend and some of his associates had problems handling these challenges. It was a privilege then and it is now to honor this warm and wonderful man, Milton Friedman.

As a gesture of our boundless regard, Pacific Institute President David Theroux would like to present Milton Friedman with this copy of the first edition, in fine condition, of the two-volume economics magnum opus by the renowned economist and classical liberal political philosopher, John Stuart Mill, *Principles of Political Economy.* This historic copy belonged to Rowland Post, the inventor of the Penny Post. Mill's *Principles* was the undisputed and most widely used text in economics in the 19th century and well into the 20th century. The volume's case is inscribed with the following:

> In deep appreciation for and recognition of your outstanding contributions to the principles of political economy and your unwavering dedication to the inseparable causes of economic prosperity and individual liberty,
>
> The Dinner Committee and Assembled Guests
> at the National Dinner to Honor Milton Friedman,
> held October 4, 1983, at the Fairmont Hotel in San Francisco,
>
> proudly present this volume,
> *Principles of Political Economy*
> by John Stuart Mill to
>
> # Milton Friedman
>
> William E. Simon, *Honorary Chairman*
> J. Peter Grace, George M. Keller, Robert H. Malott
> *Dinner Co-Chairmen*
>
> sponsored by
> The Pacific Institute for Public Policy Research
> David J. Theroux, President

PART II

Tyranny of the Status Quo

1. Tyranny of the Status Quo

Milton Friedman

Most Americans had a great surge of hope in 1980 when Ronald Reagan was elected president of the United States. Voters saw it as confirmation that "The Tide is Turning," as we labelled the final chapter of our earlier book, *Free to Choose*.[1] Ever since the New Deal, the United States had been moving in the direction of a bigger and a more intrusive government. For the first time, a man had been elected president not because he was saying what the people wanted to hear, but because the people wanted to hear what he was saying. There is an enormous difference between those two positions. Every earlier president in my lifetime was elected because he watched the polls and said what the people wanted to hear. Ronald Reagan was the first one who kept on saying the same thing for thirty years and finally it became what the people wanted to hear. That is what gave us great hope in 1980, hope that we really were going to be successful in cutting down the size of government and making for a lesser degree of interference in our lives.

To begin with, it looked as if we were getting great success. One of the first achievements of the new administration was in the energy field: the elimination of both the price ceiling on oil and the so-called entitlement program, which was a monstrous program in every respect. Opponents of a free market all threw up their hands and said, "Oh my God, the price of

---

1. Milton and Rose Friedman, *Free to Choose: A Personal Statement* (New York: Harcourt Brace Jovanovich, 1981).

gasoline and oil is going to shoot through the sky." Friends of a free market could have told them, and did, that the opposite would happen; the price came down, it didn't go up.

The president similarly had great success with Congress, which passed a series of tax cuts not as large as he initially asked for, but substantial. Furthermore, Congress accepted the idea of indexing the tax system, and cut the top rate of personal income tax from 75 to 50 percent. A number of laws were passed that supposedly were going to cut down the level of government spending. The flood of regulations that had been pouring out of the Carter administration was reduced to a trickle, and a few were even eliminated.

So for a while everything seemed fine. But then it all stalled. There have been no further gains since then. On the contrary, the level of taxes in the United States has not gone down. Taxes as a percentage of national income has stayed roughly the same or slightly increased. And more important yet, total government spending as a fraction of income has continued the upward march that has characterized it ever since the New Deal in the 1930s.

Even in the area of regulation there has been some backsliding, with the reimposition of some regulations and the creation of others by governmental agencies. Why has this happened? What has gone wrong? Why has progress seemed to be so slow? These are the questions my wife and I discuss in our forthcoming book entitled, like this article, *Tyranny of the Status Quo.*[2]

One way of approaching an explanation is by using a political generalization of very long standing and one that is vital to understanding what happens in government. A new administration, dedicated to making major change, has about six to nine months to do so. That's the honeymoon period. Once that period is over, the tyranny of the status quo asserts itself. The defeated forces regroup. The opponents of the initial measures find their voices and reorganize. And from there on, little gets accomplished.

The Franklin Delano Roosevelt administration is a good example of this political generalization. Roosevelt came into office in 1933 at a time, of course, of enormous crisis and catastrophe in the country. Recall the famous special one-hundred-day session of Congress. In that session, one

---

2. See Milton Friedman and Rose D. Friedman, *Tyranny of the Status Quo* (New York: Harcourt Brace Jovanovich, 1984).

New Deal agency after another was established: the NRA, the AAA, the PWA, the WPA. Take any three initials you can think of and they're in there—the "alphabet soup" of government agencies. After this initial spurt, the Supreme Court declared the NRA and the AAA unconstitutional, and they had to be disbanded. Roosevelt tried to pack the Supreme Court by adding to the number of judges, but the overwhelmingly democratic Congress turned him down. FDR became a victim of the tyranny of the status quo. And so it was with President Reagan. The visible changes that occurred in the early months of the Reagan administration are continuing to work their effects and have changed the atmosphere within which discussion goes on. But very few noteworthy changes have been visible thereafter.

Other more recent examples include new heads of states and new administrations elected in Britain, France, and Germany. Conservative Margaret Thatcher replaced Jim Callaghan of the Labor Party. In France, Socialist François Mitterrand replaced Gaullist Giscard d'Estaing. In Germany, Christian Democrat Helmut Kohl replaced Social Democrat Helmut Schmidt. Each case illustrates the political generalization previously mentioned. In the first six to nine months in which Margaret Thatcher was in office, she eliminated exchange controls that had been in operation for forty years, cut the top rate of the personal income tax from approximately 90 to 60 percent, and privatized the trucking industry— some very significant changes. But once that initial period was over, there were no further changes and she, like Reagan, found that total government spending which she had vowed to cut continued to increase as a fraction of income. Taxes, too, went up as a fraction of income.

François Mitterrand shows that this generalization is no respecter of ideology. A Socialist, in the first six or nine months of office he accomplished a great deal. He nationalized the banking industry, imposed heavier taxes, raised minimum wages, and imposed price and wage control over a variety of areas—changes that free market advocates regard as very bad, but changes that showed the ability of a new administration to make an impact. But then he became stymied even worse than Thatcher or Reagan. Not only did he fail to get any new measures through the French parliament, but reality forced him to take a U-turn much sharper than anything that had occurred in either Britain or the United States. The policies Mitterrand has had to adopt in the past two years are more like those of Margaret Thatcher and Ronald Reagan than of Karl Marx or John

Maynard Keynes. Three devaluations of the French franc within two years were a very clear indication of the failure of his policies. Economic reality cannot be neglected. Mitterrand was going against the basic forces of the economy, whereas Thatcher and Reagan were going along with them. As a result, the check to his policies was much greater than the check to theirs.

Moreover, Thatcher and Reagan were supported by a change in public opinion. Mitterrand was not. Despite very high unemployment in Britain, plus a severe recession, Margaret Thatcher was reelected, and reelected by an enormous parliamentary majority.

If my generalization about what leaders can accomplish in the initial period of office is accepted, Margaret Thatcher has another opportunity. In the next six or nine months she will be able to make major steps forward if she takes advantage of her opportunities. Once again there will be a honeymoon period.

Like Margaret Thatcher, Ronald Reagan may have another opportunity if he decides to run for reelection, which seems highly likely, and if he is reelected, which seems less likely. He, too, will have another opportunity to make major changes that will move this country in the direction that he would like it to go, provided he recognizes what Rose and I believe is the greatest mistake he made during his first term. When Ronald Reagan took advantage of his honeymoon, he made what seemed like bold proposals for cuts in taxes and cuts in government spending. But they weren't bold enough. If he had asked for much more, he wouldn't have gotten everything he asked for, but he would have gotten more than he did. And he would have generated no greater opposition. In my opinion, the key to success for a new administration is to take advantage of that honeymoon and make extremely bold proposals. If Reagan makes sufficiently bold proposals, if he prepares in advance a detailed program to be implemented once elected, and if he resists the temptation to make promises during the campaign that are inconsistent with his basic philosophy, he may have another chance to make a real impact.

But why is it so difficult to change things? Why is it that after an initial honeymoon everything seems to come to a halt? What is this tyranny of the status quo? The fundamental answer, I believe, comes from recognizing that, in our political system or in almost any political system, the most powerful group is not the majority but a small group in favor of a governmental program that will confer large benefits upon it at small costs to everybody else, costs that can be spread widely over the population at large. That is the group that has the greatest political power.

Let me give a very simple example. When this country was founded in 1776, nineteen out of twenty people were on farms. It took nineteen out of twenty people to grow enough food to feed themselves and the one other person. Twenty to twenty-five years ago, the number of workers and entrepreneurs on farms had shrunk to about six million out of a population close to 200 million, or less than 5 percent. In the early days of this country there were no farm support programs. But by the 1960s there were, and those farm price support programs were doling out money that amounted to something like $200 per person employed on farms. Today, twenty-three years later, there are half as many people employed on farms and the farm programs are doling out $6,000 per farm person employed. The farmers have more political clout when they are few than when they are many, and the reason is very simple. If they are few, it matters a great deal to each one of them. It pays each one of them to spend a lot of effort on trying to get a government program on his behalf. If they succeed, it will cost us something like $50 to $100 a year per person. It doesn't pay one of us to go down to Washington and lobby against the program in order to save $50 or $100. It doesn't pay us to keep informed about what happens. That is why we are ruled by a special kind of majority, a majority that is composed of a collection of minorities—3 percent who are in favor of this, 2 percent who are in favor of that. If you want to get elected to Congress, don't try to find out what the majority wants, try to build a coalition of 2 percent plus 3 percent plus 5 percent. The tyranny of the status quo is embodied in what has come to be called in Washington the "Iron Triangle."

The "Iron Triangle," like every triangle, has three corners. In one corner are the beneficiaries of the tyranny of the status quo: the farmers, the maritime industry, the automobile industry that's seeking to cut down on imports from Japan, the steel industry that's trying to prevent the American people from benefiting from cheap imported steel, and so forth. Another corner of the Iron Triangle consists of the politicians: the president, members of Congress, the state legislators, the governors. Politicians get their funds to run for election from the beneficiaries of the government programs. And the third corner, and by no means the least important, is the bureaucrats. An Iron Triangle exists in every area: in the military, among defense contractors and Congressmen who head the armed services committees, among bureaucrats, and in the Pentagon.

The issue is well illustrated by education. You would think that the beneficiary corner of education and schooling would be parents and children. They are the ones who have most at stake. But their position in the beneficiary corner has been preempted by teachers, school administrators, and teachers' unions. Why? Because teachers, school administrators, and teachers' unions are relatively few and concentrated. When government money is spent on education, each group gets what to each of them is a relatively big chunk. The parents and the students are many and dispersed. They have the most to gain or lose, but they have little to say about what goes on. Unless parents are fortunate enough to be able to send their children to private schools, they have very little to say about what goes on in the classroom. That's being determined by the professional educators. One report after another documents how terrible our educational system is, how low the quality of our schooling is, how SAT scores are going down. Why is this happening?

It's happening because our school system is centralized and bureaucratic, because it's a governmental, socialist school system. And yet what has been the reaction? The teachers' unions are saying, "You know very well the trouble. The trouble is there isn't enough money." The truth is that the amount of government money being spent per child, even after allowing for inflation, has been going up sharply. In fact, it's been going up almost as sharply as the performance of students has been going down. But nonetheless, they are one corner—and a highly effective and influential corner—of the educational Iron Triangle. Another corner, of course, is the politicians—the legislators in the state houses, the Congressmen, and the educational committees. And the third corner is the bureaucrats who administer these programs.

One of candidate Reagan's goals when he assumed office was to eliminate the newly created Department of Education. The federal government has no business playing a major role in elementary and secondary education. That should be a responsibility of the local communities. But increasingly, the federal government has been expanding its role. The Department of Education was established because the National Education Association contributed large sums to the campaign for the nomination and election of Jimmy Carter. That's putting it bluntly, but accurately and exactly. And President Reagan, quite properly, wanted to abolish it. That hasn't happened and there's no sign that it will happen. The Secretary of Education is a fine man who says all the right things, but words aren't going to solve problems.

The right solution is to eliminate centralized bureaucratic control of the public school system, of elementary and secondary schools. The best way to do that is through a voucher system under which parents will have the opportunity to choose the schools their children attend. That would substitute the principles of a private enterprise economy for the principles of a socialist economy. There is no more difficulty in understanding why our school system cannot teach our children than there is in understanding why the Russian agricultural system cannot feed its people. Both are socialist institutions, and in both cases, socialist institutions operate in the interests of the producers and not in the interests of the consumers.

The most recent Gallup poll on this subject showed that, for the first time, a majority of the people polled favor an educational voucher system: 51 percent were in favor, 38 percent opposed, 11 percent undecided. Two years ago only 43 percent favored it. In the state of California—two dedicated people in Sacramento, Roger Magyar and Leroy Chatfield—are trying to promote an initiative to introduce a voucher system for the state of California. The first attempt to get such a system approved by initiative was made years ago in Michigan, and failed. It failed, of course, because the teachers' unions, the educational bureaucracy, and the public schools, joined forces to oppose it. They will do the same in this state, and they will succeed unless the people are informed by the Pacific Institute for Public Policy Research and other organizations whose function is to educate.

What lessons can we draw from what has happened? What lessons can we draw about surmounting the tyranny of the status quo? I believe that the majority of the American people are in favor of cutting down the size of government. They are in favor of getting more control over their lives. The problem is how to make that effective. One obvious lesson is that we cannot succeed simply by electing the right people to Congress, because once the right people are elected to Congress they will proceed to do the wrong things. And they will proceed to do the wrong things because the people who elected them will demand that they do the wrong things. Let's not blame the politicians; we're the ones who are to blame. We are all of us special interests. We are all in favor of cutting down government, provided it's a government program that benefits somebody else. So that even though we all elect people to Congress because we would like to see the size of government reduced, once they are elected it is in our self-interest, understandably, to protect the special privileges that we separately enjoy. And that behavior is entirely rational. Our interest, too, is concentrated. We can hope to accomplish something by working with the small group that has the same concentrated interest. We feel—and to a considerable extent are—largely impotent in having any individual influence on broad diffused problems.

The key problem is how to arrange a package deal. The problem is most individuals would be willing to give up the special privileges they enjoy if they were confident that all the other special interests would give up theirs. But there is no way to arrange a package deal through the Congress. Congress considers each proposition separately. When each proposition is considered—for example, cutting funds for what I think to be one of the most disgraceful of all programs, namely, subsidies for higher education—what happens? You don't hear from the citizens who pay the taxes. You hear from the people who teach at those schools, you hear from the students at those schools, you hear from the concentrated special interests, and the taxpayers have no representatives.

How can we arrange a package deal? Fundamentally, there are only two ways. One is the presidential route and the other is a constitutional route. The president and the vice-president are the only people elected in this country to represent the public at large. All other officials are elected to represent a particular constituency. Therefore, a president is in a position to take a broader view, to propose package deals in the interests of the public at large. That is what Ronald Reagan did in his first year in office. It is what I hope he will do again if he is reelected in 1984.

But that solution is not, in my opinion, an effective route for the long run. A president, at most, serves for four or eight years. The bureaucracy was there before he came and will be there after he leaves. They have their fingers on all the levers of power. They are a key corner of the Iron Triangle, and are not likely to be defeated permanently by the presidential route.

The most effective way to arrange a package deal is through the Constitution. That's what the Constitution is for. The Constitution, itself, was originally drawn up as a package deal. There is hardly a provision in it that could have gotten approval from all thirteen original states if each provision had been considered separately. It was because it was a package deal in which the big states got more representation in the House of Representatives and the small states got equal representation in the Senate and so on down the line, that it was approved.

Similarly today, a constitutional amendment is a way in which we can arrange a package deal. That method is being used. For example, the National Tax Limitation Committee headed by Lewis Uhler and the National Taxpayers Union headed by James Davidson have been extraordinarily effective in promoting a constitutional amendment to balance the budget and limit the growth of taxes—the Balanced Budget and Tax Limitation Amendment. It passed the Senate by the necessary two-thirds majority last year. It passed the House by a majority, but not two-thirds. Thirty-two states now, the latest one being Missouri earlier this year, have asked Congress to call a constitutional convention to propose an amendment to balance the budget and limit spending. It would be marvelous if we could hold one. I think the first one did pretty well, and I would like to see another one. In fact, I'd love to be a delegate to such a convention. But unfortunately, it will not be held because Congress is too jealous of its powers. As a result, if a thirty-third state ratifies the amendment (thirty-four is the number required), the amendment will be passed by Congress faster than you can say "Lewis Uhler."

If the Senate and the House both pass it by a two-thirds majority, the necessary three-quarters of the states will pass it within a very short period of time. I believe that is by all odds the most effective way of trying to effect a change that will have lasting power, that will not be a momentary flash in the pan, and that will really start us on the road to cutting down the size of government.

It's not the only such amndment we need. There has been much talk about the desirability of giving the president an item veto. An item veto would make the presidential route more effective. We need a constitutional amendment to substitute a flat-rate income tax for our present monstrous income tax. Again, it will be impossible to get a true flat tax adopted by Congress, in my opinion, because if there were no loopholes in the tax laws—if there were no special privileges to be gotten through taxes, no special benefits—where would Congress raise its election funds? We also need a constitutional amendment to discipline our monetary system, enabling us to have some confidence in what a dollar will buy five, ten, fifteen, twenty years from now.

That's a pretty big agenda, but this is a pretty big country. The American people do, ultimately, control their government. They can overcome the tyranny of the status quo. Fortunately, for this country, it's the only real tyranny we have to fear at the moment. There is nothing wrong with the United States that a dose of smaller and less intrusive government would not cure.

2. Questions and Comments

Replies by Milton Friedman

How can the lesser developed countries' (LDCs') "debt bomb" be defused without turning on the printing presses and driving us into an even worse cycle of inflation?

The LDCs' debts can be defused by some banks losing a lot of money. The banks made the loans at good interest rates, and got high returns from them. I think in our system of profit and loss, we cannot possibly say that the government should bail the banks out of the bad loans they make, but allow them to keep the profits on the good ones.

Personally, I am strongly opposed to the increased quota that is being proposed for the International Monetary Fund (IMF). I believe the IMF is an organization that has no real function and ought not to exist. And that, in fact, we will do the LDCs far more harm by continuing the policies of making loans to their governments. The fundamental problem of the LDCs is that they have been centrally governmentally directed, controlled, and regulated societies. Those LDCs that have had the sense to use a market system, like Hong Kong, Singapore, and Taiwan, do not have to be bailed out; not one of them is in trouble. Which are the ones in trouble? It's the ones like Mexico, where 70 percent or more of the productive apparatus of the country is owned by the government; like Brazil and Argentina, where military governments have been controlling the economy. Those are the ones that have to be bailed out, and bailing them out only encourages them to continue policies detrimental to their citizens.

So I think the way you solve the LDC "debt bomb" problem is to require the people who make the loans to collect them. If they can, fine, and if they can't, that's their problem.

Should the Federal Reserve system be decentralized and, if so, how?

No, the Federal Reserve system should not be decentralized, it should be abolished. The Federal Reserve system is now decentralized: there are twelve Federal Reserve banks around the country and the presidents of those twelve Federal Reserve banks attend the meetings of the Open Market Investment Committee. The solution is to replace the Federal Reserve by a computer directed by a constitutional amendment.

Secretary Donald Regan says there is no connection between the federal deficit and interest rates. Would you care to comment?

The connection between the federal deficit and interest rates is small. The problem of this country is not the federal deficit but the amount of government spending. Some of the people who have done the most harm unwittingly are the fiscal conservatives who have consented to higher taxes supposedly in order to balance the budget. The only effect has been to increase government spending.

If government spending today was the same percentage of the national income as it was four years ago in 1979, we would have no deficit today. The deficit has not been created by tax cuts. The deficits have not been created because taxes are too low. The deficits have been created because government spending is too high. And the people who are crying most about the deficits today are born-again budget balancers. They are the people who have brought us our present situation, and they don't want to eliminate the deficit. What they want to do is to get higher taxes so they'll have more to spend. And the fiscal conservatives, in my opinion, will do their own cause an enormous amount of harm if they continue to stress the deficit, instead of what the real problem is—which is the level of government spending.

Will the prime rate go up or down in 1984?
What is your projection for the Dow for the end of the year?

I never predict the stock market; I follow the good example of John Pierpoint Morgan, who, when asked what the stock market would do, said, "It will fluctuate."

With respect to the prime interest rate, the answer is obviously yes. But underlying these two questions is a third: What are the prospects for the American economy in 1984? That's a question we can say something about more clearly.

Two scenarios seem possible. At the moment, it is not entirely clear which will develop. One scenario is that the economic expansion we are now in will be a short one, like 1980 to '81, and will end sometime in 1984. I think that's not unlikely. We had a monetary explosion from the middle of 1982 to the middle of 1983 with a rate of monetary growth that is higher than in any twelve-month period since World War II. That rate of monetary growth is the reason we have been having a more vigorous expansion than anybody except the monetarists predicted.

Since about July, monetary growth has tapered off and slowed down sharply. If the Fed reacts as it has reacted in the past and swings from one extreme to the other, we will have a recession sometime in 1984. That's the major source of my concern about the probability that President Reagan will be reelected. If that recession comes in the first or second quarter, there will be at the time of the election rising unemployment, rising inflation, and rising interest rates—not a scenario in which a president can be easily reelected. Should that happen, then I think the chances are very good that we will be back in a very inflationary atmosphere by 1985 or 1986, and that much of the good that has been done will be undone.

The other scenario is that we will be lucky and the Fed will not behave as it has in the past. Should it find that mystical middle ground it's always seeking and never finding, the expansion will continue throughout 1984 or at least until the third or fourth quarter of 1984, in which case the odds are pretty good that President Reagan would be reelected and that he would support lower government spending and a more restrictive monetary policy thereafter. In that case, the higher inflation in 1984, which will inevitably come, would be another blip, but we'd be headed downward.

It is very difficult to say which of those scenarios will prevail. To do so, one must be able to predict what the Federal Reserve Board will do, what the system will do, and what will come out of that machinery. I have always been much more successful in predicting the consequences of what the Fed does than in predicting what it will do.

Do you fault Mr. Reagan at all for not pushing hard enough, and is there anything specific right now that you would like to see him do or push harder for?

I believe that a president has a great deal of influence but not a great deal of power. So I don't really believe that the major fault is President Reagan's. But there are some things for which I would fault him.

The area in which I would be most critical is foreign trade. When he was here in San Francisco not long ago, he gave a talk at the Commonwealth Club, and in that talk the general statement he made about the desirability of free trade was absolutely first-rate. On the other hand, he and his administration have acceded to or promoted specific measures that are contradictory to those general principles: the so-called voluntary quotas imposed on imported Japanese cars, the enormous jump in the tariff on heavy motorcycles in order to benefit one company—Harley-Davidson—the recent measures on specialty steels from Europe, the subsidization of grain exports to Egypt. These are all absolutely contradictory to the general principle of free trade. The Administration might defend itself by claiming those actions were necessary to prevent Congress from taking even less desirable measures, but nonetheless, I wish that the administration had stood more forthrightly against those and in favor of free trade.

In general, though, I don't believe the fault is with the President. The fault is with the system, which allows, once the initial honeymoon is over, the tyranny of the status quo and the Iron Triangle to prevail.

How much of your criticism of monetary policy do you feel is the result of the fluctuations in the position of the administration and the pressure it has put on the president?

None because the Federal Reserve has behaved that way for seventy years. Moreover, to explain the immediate situation, the crucial date is October 1979; that was almost a year and a half before this administration came into power, and if you look at the pattern, it was roughly the same from October 1979 until July 1982. The pressures put on in the last half cannot possibly account for what happened in the first half.

There is a great misunderstanding about monetary policy and an enormous tendency to personalize it. So we talk about the Volcker policy, or the Reagan policy, or the Carter policy.

In almost all large organizations, the person in charge is not necessarily an appropriate indication of what's going to happen within the organization. Paul Volcker undoubtedly has a good deal of influence with the Fed, but he is only one of seven governors and one of twelve people on the Open Market Investment Committee. In addition to them, there's a large bureaucracy with a life of its own. I doubt whether there is a button Mr. Volcker could push that would make any difference.

Did not the administration, though, reappoint Mr. Volcker and did they make a mistake in reappointing him?

In reappointing Mr. Volcker? Yes, I said it at the time, I've said it before, and I've said it since: I think his reappointment suggests that the administration approves of the policy that was followed under Paul Volcker's regime.

Paul Volcker may not be to blame, but he has to be regarded as responsible for the policy that was followed. His reappointment is a clear indication that the Reagan administration approved what I believe to have been a very unfortunate monetary policy. It brought inflation down; that was a good thing. But it brought inflation down by a highly erratic monetary policy that made the accompanying recession much more severe than it otherwise would have been—by a policy that made interest rates higher than they otherwise would have been. On the whole, therefore, that was not a good monetary policy; it was a very bad one.

When Reagan outlined his economic program during the presidental campaign in September 1980, his four planks were (1) reduce government spending, (2) reduce taxes, (3) reduce regulation, and (4) maintain a stable, moderate monetary policy. But monetary policy has been anything but stable. There is no three-year period in monetary history, to the best of my knowledge, in which the growth in the quantity of money has been as *un*stable as in the period from October 1979 to October 1982. Reality did not accord with the plank in Mr. Reagan's platform. I do not believe a vote of approval should be given to a monetary administration that has departed so far from the President's fundamental desired policy.

How and when do you suggest that we go about abolishing the Federal Reserve?

That depends on how radical a reform you want to make. The simplest and perfectly feasible thing to do would be to divide the operations of the Federal Reserve into its two very different functions: (1) regulating and supervising the banking system, and (2) controlling the quantity of money. Assign the former function to the two other federal agencies that have the same function, namely the Federal Deposit Insurance Corporation and the Controller of the Currency, and have one regulatory authority. (I'm not approving of that, I'm merely responding to the question.) And then take the function of controlling the money supply and transfer that to the Treasury Department. Such a solution would be a great improvement over what you have now.

A more fundamental reform would be a constitutional amendment limiting the total quantity of non-interest-bearing money created by the federal government—whether in the form of currency or deposits—either fixing it once and for all or allowing it to grow at a specified rate. Then simply dismantle the Federal Reserve.

There are two separate issues involved here: the issue of controlling the quantity of money and the issue of what kind of regulation, if any, should control the banking system. The two raise very different problems. At the moment, I was only talking about the first of those functions.

You mentioned that if we get lucky, the economic expansion may continue into 1984; what is the most likely course of events?

The first scenario is that a recession begins in the first or second quarter of 1984, producing an economic environment in which a new president is elected. Under those circumstances, the new president would move to the traditional democratic practice of tax and tax, spend and spend, elect and elect. And that would almost surely set in motion developments that would lead to renewed inflationary prospects for 1984 and 1985. In fact, given public opposition to inflation, there would be great pressure even under those circumstances to stop it, which, in turn, might lead to renewed price and wage control.

The public's memory is relatively short. By that time, it will be over a decade since Richard Nixon made his major mistake of imposing price and wage control, and since we felt the serious consequences of that. It will be a shorter period of time since we had double-digit inflation. A new administration and Congress might very well, under those circumstances, resort to price and wage control in an attempt to suppress the inflationary pressure instead of letting it express itself openly. The result would be even worse inflation a few years later, as happened after the 1971 price controls broke down and had to be abolished. That is one possible and very unfortunate scenario.

The other scenario is that the expansion will continue through most of 1984. A new election under circumstances more favorable to the incumbent, will likely lead to a reelection of the president, who will move, as he has before, to hold down spending. With a constitutional amendment to balance the budget and limit taxes, we can gradually ratchet inflation back down.

Let me emphasize, under either case, there will be higher inflation in 1984 than in 1983. It's unavoidable because, somehow or other, this extra money that's been pumped out has to be absorbed. It's got to come out. So there will be higher inflation in 1984, but that doesn't mean it's going to be double-digit inflation. The inflation currently is running 3 to 5 percent. In the middle of 1984, I believe it will be in the neighborhood of 6 to 9 percent. That is the direction we're heading.

There was a monetary explosion from July 1982 to July 1983. The quantity of money, M–1, went up by 14 percent. A monetary expansion of 14 percent cannot be absorbed without it sooner or later coming out in the price level.

A lot of people think that the velocity of money is. . .

I wrote a piece in the *Wall Street Journal* a few weeks ago dealing exactly with that issue, and I refer you to it.

The problem with the velocity is that it went down for reasons that are perfectly understandable. At the moment, it's much more likely to go up than down, and if it goes up, it will just exacerbate the effect.

Doesn't the Fed have a problem now defining money?

Throughout the history of the Federal Reserve, every single time it has been subject to criticism because it doesn't quite know what to do, its favorite excuse is that there is a problem of defining money. That excuse is utterly irrelevant and just is *not* the case. The monetary explosion started before the new forms of bank deposits were introduced, the so-called money market accounts. The "super-NOWs" were first introduced in October 1982, again in January. But the monetary explosion started in July. The monetary explosion that started in July can't be explained by the authorization of new forms of deposit. The problem of defining money is just a smokescreen to ward off criticism.

Do you think the market is being tricked by this? Why is the market continuing to go up, if inflation is on the rise?

Because we are in a very vigorous economic expansion, there's no doubt about that. Historically, the initial stages of renewed inflation are very good for stock markets. When the stock market really zoomed back in the 1960s and '70s, it was when when we were just starting to get into this inflationary spiral. In the early stages, prices and profits go up before wages and costs go up. That's very good for the stock market. Only as that process gets underway and people start to learn what's happening and adjust to it, and wages and other costs start going up, is there an adverse effect on the market. We are currently in the first stage. We've come through a sharp disinflation and seem to be in the early stages of a reinflation. However, I do not predict that the Dow will plunge, for I don't predict anything about the stock market.

Early on in the Reagan administration, we heard talk from the supply siders about the only way to really get a handle on this inflation is perhaps to go back to the gold standard. Is that any kind of solution?

No, but there are supply siders and there are supply siders. I'm a supply sider and I never talked that way. Lots of other supply siders did not talk that way, either. Jack Kemp, Art Laffer, Jude Winniski—this small group of people did talk that way. They had overpromised on what the tax cuts would do. To have an excuse, they turned to a gold standard, an understandable human reaction. But it's not fair to label all supply siders with that view.

The United States was under a gold standard from 1879 until the first

World War, and in a modified form until 1933. That did not prevent sharp ups and downs in prices. Under the gold standard, there was a period, from 1879 to 1897, when prices were falling about 3 percent a year. From 1897 to 1914, prices went up about 50 percent. So the gold standard does not prevent sharp short-term movements. The price level was stable on an average over a long period but even in its heyday, the gold standard was not the ideal standard.

Furthermore, government establishes a gold standard, and can abolish it as well. It has done so in the past, and it would do so again. Few people who say they're for a gold standard—and Ron Paul is one of the few—are in favor of an honest-to-God gold standard in which gold is really used as money. Most advocate a *managed* gold standard. I see no reason why a government would manage a gold standard any better than it manages a paper standard. Finally, a gold standard makes real sense only if it is international. And there is no other country in the world prepared to go that way. So the suggestion is a nonstarter.

There is nothing to prevent the United States from having a gold standard in a different sense. Conrad Braun has a gold standard corporation in Kansas City. He'll hold deposits in the form of gold; checks can be written on those deposits and transferred to somebody else. There is nothing at the moment to prevent people in this country who want to from using gold as their medium of exchange. Not very many people are going to do so. For those people who are really in favor of a gold standard, that's the route they ought to take. They ought not to ask government to reestablish it. As Conrad is always saying, "The real issue is a free market and not free gold." Private people who want to operate on gold, there's nothing to stop them. And I'm all in favor of eliminating any obstacles whatsoever to private individuals transacting in whatever medium they want to. There is nothing to stop people from using Swiss francs if they want to make a deal with somebody else. And there shouldn't be. The Gold Standard Commission, established by the government, discovered that nobody was in favor of the gold standard except Ron Paul. The rest was all talk.

Are you in favor of abolishing legal tender laws?

It doesn't make a bit of difference whether they are abolished or not, for I don't think they're really of any importance.

Could you elaborate on your ideas for an improved educational system?

A voucher program is simply an arrangement in which the government, now prepared to spend roughly $3,000 a year on your child if you send him to a public school, will give you a voucher worth, let's say, $1500. You and the government split the money, and you can use that voucher to pay tuition at any school of your choice. The amendment that is going to be proposed in California would provide that such vouchers be usable in *both* public and private schools and that public schools might receive additional funds from the legislature and the local communities, but they would also receive such vouchers. The sums of money that correspond to the vouchers would be deducted from the funds public schools now receive.

The essential feature of a voucher is that parents are free to choose whether they send their children to a public school or to a private school. Currently, if you want to send your child to a private school, you pay twice for his schooling—once in the form of taxes and once in the form of tuition.

Comprehensive Bibliography

A Chronological List of Milton Friedman's
Principal Works from 1934 to the present

Books

One of the authors of *Consumer Expenditures in the United States*. Prepared for the National Resources Committee. Washington, D.C.: Government Printing Office, 1939.

With Carl Shoup and Ruth P. Mack. *Taxing to Prevent Inflation*. New York: Columbia University Press, 1943.

With Simon Kuznets. *Income from Independent Professional Practice*. New York: National Bureau of Economic Research, 1945.

Coeditor with H. A. Freeman, Frederick Mosteller, and W. Allen Wallis, and also coauthor of *Sampling Inspection*. New York: McGraw-Hill, 1948.

Essays in Positive Economics. Chicago: University of Chicago Press, 1953.

Editor of *Studies in the Quantity Theory of Money*. Chicago: University of Chicago Press, 1956.

A Theory of the Consumption Function. National Bureau of Economic Research General Series, no. 63. Princeton: Princeton University Press, 1957.

A Program for Monetary Stability. New York: Fordham University Press, 1959.

*Capitalism and Freedom. Chicago: University of Chicago Press, 1962.

Price Theory: A Provisional Text. Chicago: Aldine, 1962.

With Anna J. Schwartz. *A Monetary History of the United States, 1867–1960*. National Bureau of Economic Research Studies in Business Cycles, no. 12. Princeton: Princeton University Press, 1963.

*denotes titles specifically for the non-economist

Inflation: Causes and Consequences. Bombay: Asia Publishing House, for the Council for Economic Education, 1963.

Postwar Trends in Monetary Theory and Policy. Center for Economic Research Lecture Series, no. 5. Athens, Greece: Center for Economic Research, 1963.

With Robert V. Roosa. *The Balance of Payments: Free versus Fixed Exchange Rates.* Rational Debate Seminar. Washington, D.C.: American Enterprise Institute, 1967.

Dollars and Deficits: Inflation, Monetary Policy, and the Balance of Payments. Englewood Cliffs, N.J.: Prentice-Hall, 1968.

The Optimum Quantity of Money and Other Essays. Chicago: Aldine, 1969.

With Walter W. Heller. *Monetary vs. Fiscal Policy.* Seventh Annual Arthur K. Salomon Lecture, Graduate School of Business Administration, New York University. New York: W. W. Norton, 1969.

With Anna J. Schwartz. *Monetary Statistics of the United States.* National Bureau of Economic Research Studies in Business Cycles, no. 20. New York: Columbia University Press, 1970.

A Theoretical Framework for Monetary Analysis. National Bureau of Economic Research Occasional Paper, no. 112. New York: National Bureau of Economic Research, 1971.

*An Economist's Protest: Columns on Political Economy. Glen Ridge, N.J.: Thomas Horton & Daughters, 1972; 2d ed., 1975. (The second edition was also published in 1975 under the title *There's No Such Thing as a Free Lunch* by Open Court Publishing of LaSalle, Ill.)

**With Wilbur J. Cohen. *Social Security: Universal or Selective?* Rational Debate Seminar. Washington, D.C.: American Enterprise Institute, 1972.

Money and Economic Development. New York: Praeger, 1973.

Milton Friedman's Monetary Framework: A Debate with His Critics. Edited by Robert J. Gordon. Chicago: University of Chicago Press, 1974.

Price Theory (revised and enlarged version of *Price Theory: A Provisional Text*). Chicago: Aldine, 1976.

*Tax Limitation, Inflation and the Role of Government. Dallas, Tex.: Fisher Institute, 1978.

**With Rose D. Friedman. *Free to Choose.* New York: Harcourt Brace Jovanovich, 1980.

With Anna J. Schwartz. *From New Deal Banking Reform to World War II Inflation.* Princeton: Princeton Unversity Press, 1980.

With Anna J. Schwartz. *Monetary Trends in the United States and the United Kingdom: Their Relation to Income, Prices, and Interest Rates, 1867–1975.* Chicago: University of Chicago Press, 1982.

*Bright Promises, Dismal Performance: An Economist's Protest. Edited with an introduction by William R. Allen. New York: Harcourt Brace Jovanovich, 1983.

*denotes titles specifically for the non-economist

*With Rose D. Friedman. *Tyranny of the Status Quo: A Personal Statement.* New York: Harcourt Brace Jovanovich, 1984.

Other Publications

"Professor Pigou's Method for Measuring Elasticities of Demand from Budgetary Data." *Quarterly Journal of Economics* 1 (November 1934): 151–63.
Review of *Seasonal Variations in Industry and Trade* by Simon Kuznets. *Journal of Political Economy* 43 (December 1935): 830–32.
One of the four editors of Frank H. Knight, *The Ethics of Competition.* London and New York: George Allen & Unwin, 1935.
"Further Notes on Elasticity of Substitutions: Note on Dr. Machlup's Article." *Review of Economic Studies* 3 (February 1936): 147–48.
With Hildegarde Kneeland and Erika Schoenberg. "Plans for a Study of the Consumption of Goods and Services by American Families." *Journal of the American Statistical Association* 31 (March 1936): 135–40.
"Marginal Utility of Money and Elasticities of Demand." *Quarterly Journal of Economics* 50 (May 1936): 523–33.
Review of *Cyclical Fluctuations in Commodity Stocks* by Ralph H. Blodgett. *Journal of Political Economy* 44 (December 1936): 642–43.
Editor and minor contributor to *Studies in Income and Wealth.* Vols. 1–3. New York: National Bureau of Economic Research, 1937, 1938, and 1939.
"The Use of Ranks to Avoid the Assumption of Normality Implicit in the Analysis of Variance." *Journal of American Statistical Association* 32 (December 1937): 675–701.
"Mr. Broster on Demand Curves." *Journal of the Royal Statistical Society* 101, part 2 (1938): 450–54.
With Simon Kuznets. "Income from Independent Professional Practice, 1929–36." *National Bureau of Economic Research Bulletin*, no. 72–73 (January 1939).
Review of *The Income Structure of the United States* by Maurice Leven. *Journal of the American Statistical Association* 34 (March 1939): 224–25.
"A Comparison of Alternative Tests of Significance for the Problem of *m* Rankings." *Annals of Mathematical Statistics* 11 (March 1940): 86–92.
Review of *Business Cycles in the United States of America, 1919–32* by J. Tinbergen. American Economic Review 30 (September 1940): 657–60.
Review of *Monopolistic Competition and General Equilibrium* by Robert Triffin. *Journal of Farm Economics* 23 (February 1941): 389–90.
With W. Allen Wallis. "The Empirical Derivation of Indifference Functions."

*denotes titles specifically for the non-economist

In *Studies in Mathematical Economics and Econometrics*, pp. 175–89. Edited by O. Lange et al. Chicago: University of Chicago Press, 1942.

"Discussion of 'The Inflationary Gap' by Walter Salant." *American Economic Review* 32 (June 1942): 314–20.

"The Spendings Tax as a Wartime Fiscal Measure." *American Economic Review* 33 (March 1943): 50–62.

Review of *Saving, Investment, and National Income* by Oscar L. Altman. *Review of Economic Statistics* 26 (May 1944): 101–102.

With George J. Stigler. *Roofs or Ceilings? The Current Housing Problem.* Irvington-on-Hudson, N.Y.: Foundation for Economic Education, 1946.

"Lerner on the Economics of Control." *Journal of Political Economy* 55 (October 1947): 405–16.

"Utilization of Limited Experimental Facilities When the Cost of Each Measurement Depends on Its Magnitude." In C. Eisenhart, M. W. Hastay, and W. A. Wallis, eds., *Techniques of Statistical Analysis*, chap. 9, pp. 319–28. New York and London: McGraw-Hill, 1947.

"Planning an Experiment for Estimating the Mean and Standard Deviation of a Normal Distribution from Observation on the Cumulative Distribution." In *Techniques of Statistical Analysis*, chap. 11, pp. 339–52.

With L. J. Savage. "Planning Experiments Seeking Maxima." In *Techniques of Statistical Analysis*, chap. 13, pp. 363–72.

With Harold Hotelling, Walter Bartky, W. Edwards Deming, and Paul Hoel. "The Teaching of Statistics," a Report of the Institute of Mathematical Statistics Committee on the Teaching of Statistics. *Annals of Mathematical Statistics* 19 (March 1948): 95–115.

Review of *Cycles: The Science of Prediction* by Edward R. Dewey and Edwin F. Dakin. *Journal of the American Statistical Association* 43 (March 1948): 139–41.

Foreword to *Analysis of Wisconsin Income* by Frank A. Hanna, Joseph A. Pechman, and Sidney M. Lerner. *Studies in Income and Wealth*, vol. 9, pp. 1–16. New York: National Bureau of Economic Research, 1948.

"A Monetary and Fiscal Framework for Economic Stability." *American Economic Review* 38 (June 1948): 245–64.

With L. J. Savage. "The Utility Analysis of Choices Involving Risk." *Journal of Political Economy* 56 (August 1948): 270–304.

Discussion of "Liquidity and Uncertainty." *American Economic Review, Papers and Proceedings* 39 (May 1949): 196–201.

"'Rejoinder' to 'Professor Friedman's Proposal': Comment." *American Economic Review* 39 (September 1949): 949–55.

"The Marshallian Demand Curve." *Journal of Political Economy* 57 (December 1949): 463–95.

"Does Monopoly in Industry Justify Monopoly in Agriculture?" *Farm Policy Forum* 3 (June 1950): 5–8.

With Emile Despres, Albert G. Hart, P. A. Samuelson, and Donald H. Wallace. "The Problem of Economic Instability." *American Economic Review* 40 (September 1950): 505–38.

"Wesley C. Mitchell as an Economic Theorist." *Journal of Political Economy* 58 (December 1950): 465–93.

"Some Comments on the Significance of Labor Unions for Economic Policy." In David McCord Wright, ed., *The Impact of the Union*, pp. 204–34. New York: Harcourt Brace, 1951.

Comment on "Research in the Size Distribution of Income," a paper by Dorothy Brady. In *Conferences on Research in Income and Wealth*, pp. 55–60. *Studies in Income and Wealth*, vol. 13. New York: National Bureau of Economic Research, 1951.

Comment on "Postwar Changes in the Income of Identical Consumer Units," a paper by George Katona and Janet Fisher. In *Conference on Research in Income and Wealth*, pp. 119–22.

Comment on "A Test of an Econometric Model for the United States, 1921–1947." In *Conference on Business Cycles*, pp. 107–14. New York: National Bureau of Economic Research, 1951.

"Neoliberalism and Its Prospects." *Farmand* (Oslo, Norway) 17 February 1951, pp. 89–93.

"Commodity-Reserve Currency." *Journal of Political Economy* 59 (June 1951): 203–32.

"Comments on Monetary Policy." *Review of Economic Statistics* 33 (August 1951): 186–91.

"Les Effets d'une politique de plein emploi sur la stabilité économique: Analyse formelle," trans. Jacques Mayer. *Economie Appliquée* 4 (July–December 1951): 441–56.

"Liberté d'entreprise aux Etats-Unis." *Société Belge d'Etudes et d'Expansion Bulletin Bimestriel*, no. 148 (November–December 1951): 783–88.

"The 'Welfare' Effects of an Income Tax and an Excise Tax." *Journal of Political Economy* 60 (February 1952): 25–33.

"Price, Income, and Monetary Changes in Three Wartime Periods." *American Economic Review, Papers and Proceedings* 42 (May 1952): 612–25.

"A Reply to C. G. Phipps, 'Friedman's "Welfare" Effects.'" *Journal of Political Economy* 60 (August 1952): 334–36.

"A Method of Comparing Incomes of Families Differing in Composition." In *Conference on Research in Income and Wealth*, pp. 9–20. *Studies in Income and Wealth*, pp. 9–20. *Studies in Income and Wealth*, vol. 115. New York: National Bureau of Economic Research, 1952.

Comments. In U.S. Congress, Joint Committee on the Economic Report, *Monetary Policy and the Management of the Public Debt: Replies to Questions*. 82d Cong., 2d sess., S. Doc. no. 123, part 2. Washington, D.C., 1952. Pp. 1019–20, 1069, 1105, 1117, 1131, and 1299–1301.

With L. J. Savage. "The Expected Utility Hypothesis and the Measurability of Utility." *Journal of Political Economy* 60 (December 1952): 463–74.

Discussion on *A Survey of Contemporary Economics. American Economic Review, Papers and Proceedings* 43 (May 1953): 445–48.

"Choice, Chance, and the Personal Distribution of Income." *Journal of Political Economy* 61 (August 1953): 277–92.

"Rejoinder to Henry M. Oliver, 'Economic Advice and Political Limitations.'" *Review of Economics and Statistics* 35 (August 1953): 252.

"Why the Dollar Shortage?" *The Freeman* 4, no. 6 (December 14, 1953).

"A Reply to Martin J. Bailey, 'The Marshallian Demand Curve.'" *Journal of Political Economy* 62 (June 1954): 261–66.

"Why the American Economy is Depression Proof." *Nationalekonomiska foreningens forhandlingar* (Stockholm), no. 3 (1954): 58–77.

"The Reduction of Fluctuations in the Incomes of Primary Producers: A Critical Comment." *Economic Journal* 64 (December 1954): 698–703.

Comment on "Survey of the Empirical Evidence on Economics of Scale," a paper by Caleb Smith. In *Business Concentration and Price Policy*, pp. 230–38. A Report of the National Bureau of Economic Research. Princeton: Princeton University Press, 1955.

"Liberalism, Old Style." In *1955 Collier's Year Book*, pp. 360–63. New York, 1955.

"The Role of Government in Education." In Robert A. Solo, ed., *Economics and the Public Interest*. New Brunswick: Rutgers University Press, 1955, pp. 123–44.

"Comment." In *Income-Output Analysis: An Appraisal*. NBER Studies in Income and Wealth, vol. 18. Princeton: Princeton University Press, 1955, pp. 169–74.

"What All Is Utility?" *Economic Journal* 65 (September 1955): 405–9.

"Comment on Lloyd Ulman, 'Marshall and Friedman on Union Strength.'" *Review of Economics and Statistics* 37 (November 1955): 401–6.

"Leon Walras and His Economic System." *American Economic Review* 45 (December 1955): 900–909.

"The Quantity Theory of Money—A Restatement." In Friedman, ed., *Studies in the Quantity Theory of Money*, pp. 3–21. Chicago: University of Chicago Press, 1956.

"The Indian Alternative," comment on an article by John Strachey, *Encounter* 8 (January 1957): 71–73.

"Consumer Credit Control as an Instrument of Stabilization Policy." *Consumer Installment Credit*, vol. 2, part 2: Conference on Regulation, pp. 73–103. Washington, D.C.: National Bureau of Economic Research and the Board of Governors of the Federal Reserve System, 1957.

With Gary S. Becker. "A Statistical Illusion in Judging Keynesian Models." *Journal of Political Economy* 65 (February 1957): 64–75.

"Government Control of Consumer Credit." *University of Pennsylvania*

Bulletin, Symposium on Consumer Credit and Consumer Spending 8, no. 13 (March 25, 1957): 65–75.

"Savings and the Balance Sheet." *Bulletin of the Oxford University Institute of Statistics* 19 (May 1957): 125–36.

"Minimizing Government Control over Economic Life and Strengthening Competitive Private Enterprise." In *Problems of United States Economic Development*, vol. 1, pp. 251–57. New York: Committee for Economic Development, 1958.

"The Supply of Money and Changes in Prices and Output." In *The Relationship of Prices to Economic Stability and Growth*, pp. 241–56. 85th Cong., 2d sess., Joint Committee Print. Washington, D.C., 1958.

"Capitalism and Freedom." In Felix Morley, ed., *Essays on Individuality*. Philadelphia: University of Pennsylvania Press, 1958, pp. 168–82; 2d ed., Indianapolis: The Liberty Fund, 1977, pp. 237–58.

"Reply to Comments on A Theory of the Consumption Function." In Lincoln H. Clark, ed., *Consumer Behavior*. New York: Harper & Bros., 1958, pp. 463–70.

"Foreign Economic Aid: Means and Objectives." *Yale Review* 47 (Summer 1958): 500–516.

With Gary S. Becker. "Reply to Kuh and Johnston." *Review of Economics and Statistics* 40 (August 1958): 298.

With Gary S. Becker. "Reply [to Lawrence Klein]." *Journal of Political Economy* 66 (December 1958): 545–59.

"The Permanent Income Hypothesis: Comment." *American Economic Review* 48 (December 1958): 990–91.

"What Price Inflation?" In *Finance and Accounting* 38, part 7 (1958): 18–27.

"The Case for Flexible Exchange Rates." In *Essays on Positive Economics*, pp. 157–87. Excerpted in W. R. Allen and C. L. Allen, eds., *Foreign Trade and Finance*. New York: Macmillan, 1959, pp. 313–42.

"Discussion of 'Wage-Push Inflation,' by Walker A. Morton." At the 11th Annual Meeting of the Industrial Relations Research Association, December 1958. In *Proceedings of the Eleventh Annual Meeting of the Industrial Relations Research Association*, 1959, pp. 212–16.

Testimony (on May 25, 1959) and "The Quantity Theory of Money—A Restatement." In U.S. Congress, Joint Economic Committee, *Hearings on Employment, Growth, and Price Levels*. 86th Cong., 1st sess. pursuant to S. Con. Res. 13, part 4. Washington, D.C., 1959, pp. 605–9.

"The Demand for Money: Some Theoretical and Empirical Results." *Journal of Political Economy* 67 (August 1959): 327–51. Also published as National Bureau of Economic Research Occasional Paper, no. 68 (in 1959).

With T. W. Anderson. "A Limitation of the Optimum Property of the Sequential Probability Ratio Test." In I. Oklin et al., eds., *Contributions to Probability and Statistics*. Stanford: Stanford University Press, 1960.

"Comments." In Irwin Friend and Robert Jones, eds., *Consumption and*

Saving, vol. 2, pp. 191–206. Philadelphia: University of Pennsylvania Press, 1960.

"In Defense of Destabilizing Speculation." In Ralph W. Pfouts, ed., *Essays in Economics and Econometrics*. Chapel Hill: University of North Carolina Press, 1960, pp. 133–41.

"Vault Cash and Free Reserves." *Journal of Political Economy* 69 (April 1961): 181–82.

"Monetary Data and National Income Estimates." *Economic Development and Cultural Change* 9 (April 1961): 267–86.

"Capitalism and Freedom." *The New Individualist Review* 1 (April 1961): 3–10.

Excerpts from "Capitalism and Freedom." *Wall Street Journal*, May 1961.

"The Demand for Money." *Proceedings of the American Philosophical Society* 105 (June 1961): 259–64.

"Economic Aid Reconsidered: A Reply." *Yale Review* 50 (Summer 1961): 533–40.

"The Lag in Effect of Monetary Policy." *Journal of Political Economy* 69 (October 1961): 447–66.

"Real and Pseudo Gold Standards." *Journal of Law and Economics* 4 (October 1961): 66–79.

Review of *Inflation* by Thomas Wilson. *American Economic Review* 51 (December 1961): 1051–55.

"An Alternative to Foreign Aid." *Wall Street Journal*, April 1962.

"The Report of the Commission on Money and Credit: An Essay in *petitio principii*." *American Economic Review, Papers and Proceedings* 52 (May 1962): 291–301.

"More on Archibald versus Chicago." *Review of Economic Studies* 30, no. 1 (1962): 65–67.

"The Interpolation of Time Series by Related Series." *Journal of the American Statistical Association* 57 (December 1962): 729–57.

"Should There Be an Independent Monetary Authority?" In Leland B. Yeager, ed., *In Search of a Monetary Constitution*. Cambridge: Harvard University Press, 1962, pp. 219–43.

With David Meiselman. "The Relative Stability of Monetary Velocity and the Investment Multiplier in the United States, 1897–1958." In *Stabilization Policies*. A Series of Studies Prepared for the Commission on Money and Credit. Englewood Cliffs, N.J.: Prentice-Hall, 1963, pp. 165–268.

"Windfalls, the 'Horizon,' and Related Concepts in the Permanent-Income Hypothesis. In K. Arrow et al., *Measurement in Economics: Studies in Mathematical Economics and Econometrics in Memory of Yehuda Grunfeld*. Stanford: Stanford University Press, 1963, pp. 3–28.

With Anna J. Schwartz. "Money and Business Cycles." *Review of Economics and Statistics* 45, part 2, supplement (February 1963): 32–64.

"Exchange Rate Policy." *Swarajya* (India), March 30, 1963.

"Price Determination in the U.S. Treasury Bill Market: A Comment." *Review of Economics and Statistics* 45 (August 1963): 318–20.

"The Present State of Monetary Theory." *Economic Studies Quarterly* 14 (September 1963): 1–15.

Statement and Testimony (on November 14, 1963). In U.S., Congress, Joint Economic Committee, *Hearings on the United States Balance of Payments.* 88th Cong., 1st sess., part 3. Washington, D.C., 1963, pp. 451–59, 500–525.

"Can a Controlled Economy Work?" In *The Conservative Papers.* Garden City, N.Y.: Doubleday, Anchor Books, 1964, pp. 162–74.

Statement and Testimony (on March 3, 1964). In U.S., Congress, House, Committee on Banking and Currency, *Hearings on the Federal Reserve System after Fifty Years,* before the Subcommittee on Domestic Finance. 88th Cong., 2d sess. Washington, D.C., 1964. Vol. 2, pp. 1133–78, 1220–22.

"Postwar Trends in Monetary Theory and Policy." *National Banking Review* 2 (September 1964): 1–9.

"The Goldwater View of Economics." *New York Times Magazine,* October 11, 1964.

"Comment on 'Collusion in the Auction for Treasury Bills.'" *Journal of Political Economy* 72 (October 1964): 513–14.

With David Meiselman. "Keynes and the Quantity Theory: Reply to Donald Hester." *Review of Economics and Statistics* 46 (November 1964): 369–76.

"A Program for Monetary Stability." In Marshall D. Ketchum and Leon T. Kendall, eds., *Readings in Financial Institutions.* Boston: Houghton Mifflin, 1965, pp. 189–209.

Foreword to *Determinants and Effects of Changes in the Stock of Money, 1875–1960* by Phillip Cagan. National Bureau of Economic Research Studies in Business Cycles, no. 13. New York: Columbia University Press, 1965, pp. xxiii–xxviii.

"Social Responsibility: A Subversive Doctrine." *National Review,* August 24, 1965, pp. 721–24.

"Economic Libertarianism: Part I." In *Proceedings of the Conference on Savings and Residential Financing,* 1965, pp. 10–29.

With David Meiselman. "Reply to Ando and Modigliani and to DePrano and Mayer." *American Economic Review* 55 (September 1965): 753–85.

"Transfer Payments and the Social Security System." *National Industrial Conference Board Record,* September 1965, pp. 7–10.

"The Lessons of U.S. Monetary History and Their Bearing on Current Policy." Memorandum prepared for Consultants Meeting, Board of Governors of the Federal Reserve System, October 7, 1965.

"What Price Guideposts?" In George P. Shultz and Robert Z. Aliber, eds.,

Guidelines, Informal Controls and the Market Place. Chicago: University of Chicago Press, 1966, pp. 17–39.

With Yale Brozen. *The Minimum Wage: Who Pays?* Washington, D.C.: The Free Society Association, 1966.

Communication on "A Free Market in Education." *The Public Interest*, no. 3 (Spring 1966): 107.

"Why Does the Free Market Have Such a Bad Press?" *Human Events* (Washington, D.C.), July 2, 1966, pp. 8, 14.

"A Tax Subsidy for the Poor?" *Social Service Outlook* 1 (April 1966): 13–14.

"Current Monetary Policy." Memorandum prepared for Consultants Meeting, Board of Governors of the Federal Reserve System, June 15, 1966.

"Interest Rates and the Demand for Money." *Journal of Law and Economics* 9 (October 1966): 71–85.

What Should Monetary and Fiscal Policy Be in the Present Situation? A Symposium at the Twentieth Annual Conference of Bank Correspondents, First National Bank of Chicago, November 22, 1966.

The Case for the Negative Income Tax: A View from the Right. Talk given at the National Symposium on Guaranteed Income sponsored by the U.S. Chamber of Commerce, Washington, D.C., December 9, 1966.

"Why Not a Voluntary Army?" In Sol Tax, ed., *The Draft: A Handbook of Facts and Alternatives.* (Based on a conference held at the University of Chicago, December 4–7, 1966). Chicago: University of Chicago Press, 1967, pp. 200–207.

"Value Judgments in Economics." In Sidney Hook, ed., *Human Values and Economic Policy.* New York: New York University Press, 1967, pp. 85–93.

"L'Economie politique des accords monetaires internationaux" ("The Political Economy of International Monetary Arrangements"). In Emil M. Claassen, ed., *Les Fondements philosophiques des systèmes économiques* (Essays in Honor of Jacques Rueff). Paris: Payot, 1967, pp. 384–94.

"The Case for the Negative Income Tax." *National Review*, March 7, 1967, pp. 239–41.

"Must We Choose Between Inflation and Unemployment?" *Stanford Graduate School of Business Bulletin* 35 (Spring 1967): 10–13, 40, 42.

"Myths That Keep People Hungry." *Harper's Magazine*, April 1967, pp. 16–24. Also published separately as a pamphlet in 1968 by the Forum of Free Enterprise, Bombay, India.

"The Case for Abolishing the Draft—and Substituting for It an All-Volunteer Army." *New York Times Magazine*, May 14, 1967.

"The Monetary Theory and Policy of Henry Simons." (The Third Henry Simons Lecture, delivered at the Law School, University of Chicago, May 5, 1967.) *Journal of Law and Economics* 10 (October 1967): 1–13.

"Taxes, Money and Stabilization." *Washington Post*, November 5, 1967, pp. H1, H3.

Statement and Testimony (on February 1, 1968). In U.S., Congress, Senate, Committee on Banking and Currency. *Hearings on the Gold Cover*, on S. 1307, S. 2815, and S. 2857 relating to repeal of the gold reserve requirements for U.S. currency. 90th Cong., 2d sess. Washington, D.C., 1968, pp. 152–66.

"Has the New Economics Failed? An Interview with Milton Friedman." *Dun's Review*, February 1968, pp. 38–39, 93–94, 96.

"The Role of Monetary Policy." (Presidential Address, American Economic Association, December 29, 1967). *American Economic Review* 58 (March 1968): 1–17.

"Money and the Interest Rate." Address before the University of Miami Savings Institutions Forum, March 11, 1968. In *Proceedings of the University of Miami Savings Institution Forum*, 1968.

"The Higher Schooling in America." *The Public Interest*, no. 11 (Spring 1968), pp. 108–12.

"Factors Affecting the Level of Interest Rates." *Proceedings of the Conference on Savings and Residential Financing*, 1968, pp. 11–27.

"Money: Quantity Theory." In *International Encyclopedia of the Social Sciences*, 1968 ed., pp. 432–47.

"The Case for the Negative Income Tax." In Melvin R. Laird, ed., *Republican Papers*. New York: Praeger, 1968, pp. 202–20.

With A. J. Schwartz. "The Definition of Money: Net Wealth and Neutrality as Criteria." *Journal of Money, Credit, and Banking* 1 (February 1969): 1–14.

"Worswick's Criticism of the Correlation Criterion, A Comment." *Journal of Money, Credit, and Banking* 1 (August 1969): 506.

"The Euro-Dollar Market: Some First Principles." *The Morgan Guaranty Survey*, October 1969, pp. 4–15.

"The Schizophrenic Businessman: Friend and Enemy of Free Enterprise." Paper prepared for the International University for Presidents, Young Presidents' Organization, Phoenix, Arizona, April 25, 1966. In Leonard Silk, ed., *Readings in Contemporary Economics*. New York: McGraw-Hill, 1970, pp. 27–35.

Statement and Testimony (on October 6, 1969), and Answers to Supplementary Questions Submitted Later. In U.S. Congress, Joint Economic Committee, *Hearings on Economic Analysis and the Efficiency of Government*, before the Subcommittee on Economy in Government, 91st Cong., 1st sess., part 3. Washington, D.C., 1970, pp. 810–29, 873–78.

Statement and Testimony on Family Assistance Programs (on November 7, 1969). In U.S., Congress, House, Committee on Ways and Means, *Hearings on Social Security and Welfare Proposals*. 91st Cong., 1st sess., part 6. Washington, D.C., 1970, pp. 1944–57.

The Counter-Revolution in Monetary Theory. IEA Occasional Paper, no. 33. London: Institute of Economic Affairs, 1970.

"The Market vs. the Bureaucrat." In Abraham Kaplan, ed., *Individuality and the New Society*. Seattle: University of Washington Press, 1970, pp. 69–88.

"Controls on Interest Rates Paid by Banks." *Journal of Money, Credit, and Banking* 2 (February 1970): 15–32.

"Monetary Policy for a Developing Society." *Bank Markazi Iran Bulletin* 9 (March-April 1970): 700–712.

"A Theoretical Framework for Monetary Analysis." *Journal of Political Economy* 78 (March-April 1970): 193–238.

"Comment on Tobin." *Quarterly Journal of Economics* 84 (May 1970): 318–27.

"Special Interest and the Law." *Chicago Bar Record*, June 1970, pp. 434–41.

"We *Must* Stand Firm Against Inflation." *Reader's Digest*, June 1970, pp. 202–4, 206.

"Social Responsibility of Business." *New York Times Magazine*, September 13, 1970.

"The New Monetarism: Comment." *Lloyds Bank Review*, no. 98 (October 1970), pp. 52–53.

"Money, Economic Activity, Interest Rates: The Outlook." In *Savings and Loan Annals, 1970*. Chicago: U.S. Savings and Loan League, 1971, pp. 60–68.

"A Monetary Theory of Nominal Income." *Journal of Political Economy* 79 (March-April 1971): 323–37.

"Is a Nation Justified in Compelling Physical Servitude from an Individual?" Interview in *The Montana Review* (University of Montana) 73 (April 16, 1971): 8–10.

"The Dollar Standard: Its Problems and Prospects." *Montana Business Quarterly* 9 (Spring 1971): 5–12.

"Government Revenue from Inflation." *Journal of Political Economy* 79 (July-August 1971): 846–56.

Statement and Testimony (on September 23, 1971). In U.S., Congress, Joint Economic Committee, *Hearings on the President's New Economic Program*. 92d Cong., 1st sess., part 4. Washington, D.C., 1971, pp. 698–706, 716–43.

"Morality and Controls" (I and II). *New York Times*, October 28 and 29, 1971, p. 39M.

"The Need for Futures Markets in Currencies." Prepared for the Chicago Mercantile Exchange, Fall 1971. In *The Futures Market in Foreign Currencies*. Chicago: International Monetary Market of the Chicago Mercantile Exchange, 1972, pp. 6–12.

"A Libertarian Speaks." Interview in *Trial: The National Legal Newsmagazine*, January-February 1972, pp. 22–24.

"Monetary Trends in the United States and the United Kingdom." *The American Economist* 16 (Spring 1972): 4–17.

"Milton Friedman Responds." Interview in *Business and Society*, no. 1 (Spring 1972), pp. 5–16.

"Have Monetary Policies Failed?" *American Economic Review, Papers and Proceedings* 62 (May 1972): 11–18.

"Social Security: The Poor Man's Welfare Payment to the Middle Class." *The Washington Monthly*, May 1972, pp. 11–13.

"Monetary Policy." *Proceedings of the American Philosophical Society* 116 (June 1972): 183–96.

"Comments on the Critics." *Journal of Political Economy* 80 (September-October 1972): 906–50.

"Monetary Policy in Developing Countries." In Paul A. David and Melvin W. Reder, eds., *Nations and Households in Economic Growth: Essays in Honor of Moses Abramovitz*. New York: Academic Press, 1974, pp. 265–78.

"How Much Monetary Growth?" *Morgan Guaranty Survey*, February 1973, pp. 5–10.

"Interview: Milton Friedman." *Playboy*, February 1973.

"Contemporary Monetary Problems." *Economic Notes* (Monte dei Paschi di Siena) 2 (1973): 5–18.

"See Yourself as V.I.P.'s See You: Milton Friedman." Interview in *Medical Economics*, April 16, 1973.

"Milton Friedman–Sir Dennis Robertson Correspondence." *Journal of Political Economy* 81 (July–August 1973): 1033–39.

"The Voucher Idea." *New York Times Magazine*, September 23, 1973. Reprinted in *An Economist's Protest*, 2d ed.

How Well Are Fluctuating Exchange Rates Working? AEI Reprint, no. 18. Washington, D.C.: American Enterprise Institute, October 1973. Reprint of text of statement before the Subcommittee on International Exchange and Payments, Joint Economic Committee, U.S. Congress, June 21, 1973.

"A Simple Idea Whose Time Has Come: Proposed California Amendment Would Allow Citizens to Limit Taxes." *Manion Forum* (South Bend, Ind.), October 28, 1973.

"Facing Inflation." Interview in *Challenge*, November–December 1973, pp. 29–37.

Living with Inflation: Three Essays. AEI Reprint, no. 23. Washington, D.C.: American Enterprise Institute, March 1974.

"Monetary Policy: A Letter (II)." Federal Reserve Bank of St. Louis *Review* 56 (March 1974): 20–23.

"A Bias in Current Measures of Economic Growth." *Journal of Political Economy* 82, part 1 (March-April 1974): 431–32.

"Commentary." In *International Inflation: Four Commentaries*, pp. 12–18. A panel discussion with Andrew Brimmer, George Freeman, and Helmut Schlesinger, under the auspices of the Federal Reserve System's Committee on International Research and Analysis, held at the Federal Reserve Bank of

Chicago, December 3–4, 1973. Chicago: Federal Reserve Bank of Chicago, July 1974.

"Using Escalators to Help Fight Inflation." *Fortune*, July 1974, pp. 94–97, 174, 176.

Indexing and Inflation. An AEI Round Table with Charles Walker, Robert J. Gordon, and William Fellner, held July 17, 1974. Washington, D.C.: American Enterprise Institute, 1974.

Monetary Correction. IEA Occasional Paper, no. 41. London: Institute of Economic Affairs, 1974.

"Inflation, Taxation, and Indexation." In *Inflation: Causes, Consequences, Cures*. IEA Readings, no. 14. London: Institute of Economic Affairs, 1974, pp. 71–88.

"Money." In *Encyclopedia Britannica*, 15th ed. (1974), pp. 349–56.

Free Markets for Free Men. Selected Paper no. 45. Chicago: University of Chicago, Graduate School of Business, [November] 1974.

"An Interview with Milton Friedman." *Reason*, December 1974, pp. 4–14.

Is Inflation a Curable Disease? Alex C. Walker Memorial Lecture, December 5, 1974. Pittsburgh: Published jointly by the Pittsburgh National Bank, Alex C. Walker Educational and Charitable Foundation and the University of Pittsburgh Graduate School of Business, 1975.

"The National Business Outlook for 1975." Delivered at a one-day conference cosponsored by the School of Business Administration of Portland State University and the Portland Chamber of Commerce in cooperation with the Harvard and Stanford Business School Associations, Portland, Oregon, December 16, 1974. In *Proceedings of the 12th Annual Business and Economic Outlook for 1975*, pp. 1–27.

Inflation and the American Economy. Speech before the Economic Club of Indianapolis, January 9, 1975. Indianapolis: Economic Club, 1975.

"Myth and Reality in Contemporary Public Opinion." William Arthur Maddox Memorial Lecture delivered at Rockford College, December 6, 1974. In *Widening Horizons* (Rockford College), vol. 11, no. 3 (March 1975).

Milton Friedman in Australia, 1975. Sydney: Constable & Bain and the Graduate Business Club, 1975. Transcripts of two talks delivered in Sydney: "Inflation and the Management of Western Economics" (April 1, 1975) and "Can Inflation Be Cured. . .Before It Ends Free Society?" (April 2, 1975).

"Twenty-five Years after the Rediscovery of Money: What Have We Learned? Discussion." *American Economic Review, Papers and Proceedings* 65 (May 1975): 176–79.

"Rich and Poor." In John Vaizey, ed., *Whatever Happened to Equality?* London: The British Broadcasting Corporation, 1975.

With John Exter. "The Role of Value of Gold: Two Views." *Reason*, special financial issue (June 1975), pp. 86–94. (Based on "Gold—Its Value as

Money and an Inflation Hedge," remarks given at the Third Annual Monetary and Trade Outlook Conference of the International Monetary Market, Chicago Mercantile Exchange, October 16, 1974.)

Unemployment versus Inflation? An Evaluation of the Phillips Curve. IEA Occasional Paper, no. 44. London: Institute of Economic Affairs, 1975.

"The Future of Capitalism." *Student Conference on National Affairs XX Proceedings* (Texas A&M University), 1975, pp. 6–9.

"Five Examples of Fed Double-Talk." *Wall Street Journal*, August 21, 1975.

"Regulation Foe: Milton Friedman Tells Why He Is Against [State Control of Hospital Rates]." Interview in *The Investor-Owned Hospital Review* 8 (August-September 1975): 16–17.

"Gold, Money and the Law: Comments." In Henry G. Manne and Roger LeRoy Miller, eds., *Gold, Money and the Law.* Chicago: Aldine Publishing Co. for the Center for Studies in Law and Economics of the University of Miami Law School, 1975, pp. 71–81.

Testimony and Prepared Statement (on November 6, 1975). In U.S., Congress, Senate, Committee on Banking, Housing and Urban Affairs, *Hearings on Oversight on the Conduct of Monetary Policy Pursuant to House Concurrent Resolution 133.* 94th Cong., 1st sess. Washington, D.C., 1975, pp. 34–49.

"There's No Such Thing as a Free Lunch. . .Ever!" Interview in the *Hillsdale Collegian*, December 4, 1975, pp. 6–8.

Testimony and Prepared Statement (on October 20, 1975). In U.S., Congress, Joint Economic Committee, *Hearings on Jobs and Prices in Chicago.* 94th Cong., 1st sess. Washington, D.C., 1976, pp. 45–50.

Testimony and Prepared Statement (on January 22, 1976). In U.S., Congress, House, Committee on Banking, Currency and Housing, *Hearings on Financial Institutions and the Nation's Economy (FINE): "Discussion Principles,"* before the Subcommittee on Financial Institutions, Supervision, Regulation and Insurance. 94th Cong., 1st and 2d sess., part 3. Washington, D.C., 1976, pp. 2151–92.

Comment: "Are Externalities Relevant?" In E. G. West, *Nonpublic School Aid: The Law, Economics, and Politics of American Education.* Lexington, Mass.: D. C. Heath, Lexington Books, 1976, pp. 92–93.

The Future of the American Economy. Bicentennial Lecture of the American Experience Program, University of Pittsburgh. Pittsburgh: University of Pittsburgh, February 1976.

With Anna J. Schwartz. "From Gibson to Fisher." *Explorations in Economic Research* 3 (Spring 1976): 288–91.

"In His Own Words: Economist Milton Friedman Calls the Income Tax 'An Unholy Mess' and Wants to Reform It." Interview in *People Weekly* 5 (April 5, 1976): 49–52.

Comment on "Long Run Effects of Fiscal and Monetary Policy on Aggregate

Demand," by James Tobin and Willem Buiter. In Jerome L. Stein, ed., *Monetarism*. Amsterdam and New York: North Holland Publishing, 1976, pp. 310–17.

Foreword to Fritz Machlup, ed., *Essays on Hayek*. New York: New York University Press, 1976, pp. xxi–xxiv.

Meyer Feldberg et al., eds., *Milton Friedman in South Africa*. Cape Town: University of Cape Town Graduate School of Business, and Johannesburg: The Sunday Times, 1976.

"The Milton Friedman View" (sample of comments during March 22-April 5, 1976 visit to South Africa). *University of Cape Town Graduate School of Business Journal*, 1975–76, pp. 15–18.

"The Fragility of Freedom." In *Brigham Young University Studies* 16 (Summer 1976): 561–74.

"Interview with Economist Milton Friedman." *Christian Science Monitor*, August 26, 1976, p. 17.

Letter of July 11, 1976 to Senator Jesse Helms (on the Gold Clause Amendment), *Congressional Record* 122, no. 148, part 2 (September 28, 1976): S 1691.

"Strategy for Business." *Boardroom Reports* (New York), October 30, 1976, pp. 3–4.

"Homer Jones: A Personal Reminiscence." *Journal of Monetary Economics* 2 (November 1976): 433–36.

"Milton Friedman Speaks." *World Research* INK (San Diego) 1 (December 1976): 1–4.

Adam Smith's Relevance for 1976. Introduction by Joseph J. Spengler. IIER Original Paper, no. 5. Los Angeles: International Institute for Economic Research, December 1976.

From Galbraith to Economic Freedom. Preface by Arthur Seldon. IEA Occasional Paper, no. 49. London: Institute for Economic Affairs, January 1977.

"Payroll Taxes, No; General Revenue, Yes." In *The Crisis in Social Security: Problems and Prospects*. San Francisco: Institute for Contemporary Studies, 1977, pp. 25–30.

"The Nobel Prize in Economics, 1976" (a talk about receiving the Nobel Prize, delivered at the Income Distribution Conference sponsored by the Hoover Institution, January 29, 1977). Stanford: Hoover Institution, 1977.

"The Future of Capitalism" (a talk delivered at Pepperdine University, February 9, 1977). Malibu, Calif.: Pepperdine University, 1977. Reprinted in *Tax Limitation, Inflation and the Role of Government*.

"Where Carter Is Going Wrong: Interview with Nobel Prize Winning Milton Friedman." *U.S. News & World Report*, 7 March 1977, pp. 20–22.

"Containing Spending." *Society* (Transaction, Inc., Rutgers University) 14 (March–April 1977): 89–92.

With Franco Modigliani. "Discussion of 'The Monetarist Controversy.'"
  Federal Reserve Bank of San Francisco Economic Review, supplement
  (Spring 1977), pp. 12–26.
"Cost Effectiveness in Health Care Takes Competition, Friedman Thinks."
  Interview in *Review: The Magazine for Hospital Management* 10, no. 2
  (April 1977): 22–24.
The Source of Strength (speech delivered before the Presidents' Club of
  Michigan General Corporation, New Orleans, April 2, 1977). Dallas:
  Michigan General Corporation, May 1977.
"Monetary Policy and the Inflation Rate." Letter to the Editor, *The Times*
  (London), 2 May 1977.
"Milton Friedman, the Chilean Junta and the Matter of Their Association" (an
  exchange of letters among Nobel laureates: Friedman with Baltimore and
  Luria, and with Wald and Pauling). *New York Times*, 22 May 1977, sec. 4,
  p. 18.
"Inflation and Unemployment" (Nobel Lecture). *Journal of Political Economy*
  85 (June 1977): 451–72. Also published as Occasional Paper no. 51 of the
  Institute of Economic Affairs (London, May 1977), and in *Les Prix Nobel en
  1976* (Stockholm: The Nobel Foundation, 1977).
"A Look at Carter Economics." *Alaska Business Trends*. Anchorage: Alaska
  Pacific Bank, July 1977, pp. 4–10.
"*Reason* Interview: Milton Friedman." *Reason* (August 1977): 24–29.
"The Economy and You: What Lies Ahead?" *Stanford Magazine* 5 (Fall/Winter
  1977–78): 22–27.
"Liberal McCarthyism: A Personal Experience." *The Commonwealth*,
  21 November 1977, pp. 490–94.
"Time Perspective in Demand for Money." *Scandinavian Journal of Economics*
  79, no. 4 (1977): 397–417.
"Capitalism, Socialism, and Democracy: A Symposium." *Commentary* 65
  (April 1978): 39–41.
"Has the Tide Turned?" *The Listener* (London) 99 (27 April 1978): 526–28.
"The Limitations of Tax Limitation." *Policy Review*, Summer 1978, pp. 7–14.
"Relying on the Free Market." Letter to the Editor, *The Times* (London), 15
  August 1978.
Milton Friedman Gives the Answers. Buena Park, Calif.: Americanism
  Educational League, August 1978.
"Milton Friedman on Floating Rates." Letter to the Editor, *Wall Street Journal*,
  28 August 1978.
"Needed: An Investigative Report on Investigative Reporting." *Taxing &
  Spending* 1, no. 1 (October–November 1978): 15.
A special series of 12 articles in the *San Francisco Chronicle*, 23 and 30
  January; 6, 13, 20, and 27 February; 6, 13, 20, and 27 March; 3 and 10
  April 1979.

Interview (by Harry Farrell). *San Jose Mercury News*, 11–13 February 1979 (a three-part series).

"The Economics of Free Speech." *Ordo*, Band 30 (1979), pp. 221–27.

"Correspondence with Milton Friedman: A Debate on Britain's Policy." *Director* (London), December 1979.

"Prices of Money and Goods Across Frontiers: The £ and $ Over a Century." *The World Economy* 2 (February 1980): 497–511.

"Monetarism: A Reply to the Critics." *The Times* (London), 3 March 1980.

"The Economic Responsibility of Government," pp. 5–14. In *Milton Friedman and Paul Samuelson Discuss the Economic Responsibility of Government.* College Station, Tex.: Texas A&M University, Center for Education and Research in Free Enterprise, 1980.

Memorandum to U.K. Treasury and Civil Service Committee on "Enquiry into Monetary Policy," 11 June 1980. In Great Britain, House of Commons (1979–80), vol. 720, part 1 (July 1980), pp. 55–61.

"Japan—Free to Choose?" *Look Japan*, 10 November 1980, pp. 6–7, 9.

"America: Its Economy and Government." *The Commonwealth* 74, no. 45 (10 November 1980): 243–44, 247.

"The Changing Character of Financial Markets." In Martin Feldstein, ed., *The American Economy in Transition.* Chicago: University of Chicago Press, 1980, pp. 78–86.

"A Memorandum to the Fed." *Wall Street Journal*, 30 January 1981, p. 18.

The Invisible Hand in Economics and Politics. Singapore: Institute of Southeast Asian Studies, 1981.

Introduction to *New Individualist Review.* A Periodical Reprint. Indianapolis: Liberty Press, 1981.

Introduction to *Midnight Economist: Choices, Prices, and Public Policy*, by William R. Allen. New York: Playboy Press, 1981.

Foreword to *Markets and Minorities*, by Thomas Sowell. New York: Basic Books, 1981.

Market Mechanisms and Central Economic Planning. Washington, D.C.: American Enterprise Institute, 1981.

With Michael Porter, Fred Gruen, and Don Stammer. *Taxation, Inflation, and the Role of Government.* Centre for Independent Studies Occasional Paper, no. 4. St. Leonards, N.S.W., Australia: Centre for Independent Studies, June 1981.

"Conscription Study Already Drafted." Letter to the Editor, *Wall Street Journal*, 11 June 1981.

"The Market and Human Freedom." *Private Practice*, July 1981, pp. 36–37, 42–44, 46.

"Money Supply's Link to the Economy." Letter to the Editor, *Wall Street Journal*, 30 July 1981.

"Milton Friedman on Reaganomics." Interview in *Human Events*, 5 December 1981, pp. 1, 6–9.

"The Federal Reserve and Monetary Instability." *Wall Street Journal*, 1 February 1982.

"Monetary Policy: Theory and Practice." *Journal of Money, Credit, and Banking* 14 (February 1982): 98–118.

With Anna J. Schwartz. "The Effect of the Term Structure of Interest Rates on the Demand for Money in the United States." *Journal of Political Economy* 90 (February 1982): 201–12.

"Erratic Pulse of the Money Supply." Letter to the Editor, *Wall Street Journal*, 28 June 1982.

"Current Economic and Political Developments in the United States." *Focus* (Fraser Institute), no. 1 (July 1982): 5–19.

"Monetary Policy: Theory and Practice. A Reply." *Journal of Money, Credit, and Banking* 14 (August 1982): 404–6.

"Supply-Side Policies: Where Do We Go from Here?" In *Supply-Side Economics in the 1980s: Conference Proceedings*, pp. 53–63. Westport, Conn.: Quorum Books, 1982.

"Washington: Less Red Ink." *The Atlantic*, February 1983, pp. 18, 20–24, 26.

"A Monetarist View," pp. 1–17. In Alan Horrox and Gillian McCredie, eds., *Money Talks: Five Views of Britain's Economy*. London: Thames Television, 1983.

"The Real Threat to U.S. Security." *The Commonwealth* 72, no. 1 (25 April 1983): 120–21, 124.

"A Monetarist Reflects." Contribution to the Keynes Centenary of *The Economist*, 4 June 1983, pp. 17–19.

Away from Collectivism. . .Toward Freedom! Buena Park, Calif.: Americanism Educational League, 1983.

"Monetary Variability: United States and Japan." *Journal of Money, Credit, and Banking* 15 (August 1983): 339–43.

About the Authors

Milton Friedman is a senior fellow of the Hoover Institution, Stanford University, professor emeritus of economics at the University of Chicago, and 1976 Nobel laureate in economic science. (See Introduction, pages 1–7 for his complete biography.)

M. Bruce Johnson has been the Research Director for the Pacific Institute and is Chairman of the Institute's Board of Academic Advisors. He is professor of economics at the University of California, Santa Barbara, and past president of the Western Economics Association. He has taught at the University of Washington, UCLA, and the University of Miami. Dr. Johnson received his B.A. from Carleton College and his M.A. and Ph.D. in economics from Northwestern University. A contributor to numerous scholarly volumes and journals, he is the author or editor of nine books including three from the Pacific Institute, *Forestlands: Public and Private* (with R. Deacon), *Resolving the Housing Crisis*, and *Rights and Regulation* (with T. Machan).

George M. Keller has been Chairman and Chief Executive Officer of Chevron Corporation since 1981. A graduate of Massachusetts Institute of Technology in chemical engineering, he is a Director of First Interstate Bancorporation and serves as a Trustee of MIT, Notre Dame College,

American Enterprise Institute, American Petroleum Institute, and Council on Foreign Relations.

Benjamin Stein is a regular columnist for the *Los Angeles Herald Examiner*. The author of nine books including four novels, he is also a TV comedy writer and the author of numerous screenplays. An economist by training, he studied under Milton Friedman at Columbia University, and his parents, the well-known economist Herbert and his wife Mildred Stein, were fellow graduate students with Dr. Friedman. Ben Stein received his law degree from Yale University, and he is a regular contributor to the *Wall Street Journal*, *Washington Post*, and many other publications.

David J. Theroux is the president of the Pacific Institute for Public Policy Research. Formerly vice president and director of academic affairs for the Cato Institute, Mr. Theroux received his M.B.A. from the University of Chicago and holds three degrees in engineering and mathematics from the University of California at Berkeley. He has been senior editor of *Policy Report* and editor of the scholarly monograph series, *Cato Papers*. He is the author of *Freedom on Film* (with M. Mueller), and the editor of *The Energy Crisis: Government and the Economy*, and *Private Rights and Public Lands* (with P. Truluck). His articles and reviews have appeared in *Economic Affairs*, *Insight*, *Libertarian Review*, *Los Angeles Herald Examiner*, *Los Angeles Times*, *Manchester Union Leader*, *Oakland Tribune*, *Santa Ana Register*, *St. Louis Post Dispatch*, *USA Today*, and many other publications.